EBURY PRESS

DR MATHAI'S ABC TO HEALTH

A second-generation homeopathic physician, Dr Issac Mathai is a world-renowned holistic health consultant treating patients from more than eighty countries over the last thirty years. He studied Chinese pulse diagnosis and acupuncture at the WHO Institute, Nanjing, China, learnt yoga and transcendental meditation, and has participated in the Mind–Body Medicine programme of Harvard Medical School, USA. His rich experience started with interning with his mother, Dr Annamma Mathai, and working at speciality clinics, including Europe's first and largest holistic health clinic, the 101 Clinic. He is a visiting consultant at holistic clinics in London, New York and Washington, DC. Having addressed several conferences worldwide on holistic health, he has been invited by the World Health Organization into its committee for 'The Renewal of the Global Health Policy for the 21st Century'. He has treated people ranging from the royalty of the UK, the Middle East and India to Nobel laureate Archbishop Desmond Tutu, famous singers, industrialists, CEOs, villagers and tribals. His dream of offering holistic integrative medicine to all is being fulfilled through his establishments—the SOUKYA International Holistic Health Centre, the SAHAYA Holistic Integrative Hospital and his SOUKYA Foundation-run free clinics and charity centres.

DR MATHAI'S ABC TO HEALTH

Your Complete Dictionary to Everyday Wellness

EBURY PRESS

An imprint of Penguin Random House

EBURY PRESS

USA | Canada | UK | Ireland | Australia
New Zealand | India | South Africa | China | Singapore

Ebury Press is part of the Penguin Random House group of companies
whose addresses can be found at global.penguinrandomhouse.com

Published by Penguin Random House India Pvt. Ltd
4th Floor, Capital Tower 1, MG Road,
Gurugram 122 002, Haryana, India

Penguin Random House India

First published in Ebury Press by Penguin Random House India 2023

10 9 8 7 6 5 4 3 2 1

The views and opinions expressed in this book are the author's own and the facts are as reported by him which have been verified to the extent possible, and the publishers are not in any way liable for the same.

ISBN 9788184007893

Typeset in Sabon LT Std by MAP Systems, Bengaluru, India
Printed at Repro India Limited

www.penguin.co.in

FSC www.fsc.org MIX Paper from responsible sources FSC® C047271

This is a legitimate digitally printed version of the book and therefore might not have certain extra finishing on the cover.

Contents

Introduction

It was one of those meetings in 2020, when Dr Issac Mathai and I were engaged in a general discussion on the state of healthcare in India, especially in the context of the pandemic. We discussed various issues on why some succumbed, while others survived COVID, we discussed the lifestyle of the current generation in contrast to the previous two generations and we discussed the eating and sleeping habits of the current generation.

As a journalist, what caught my attention was Dr Mathai's repeated reference to prevention and daily wellness, which eventually contributes to great health in the long run.

He was persistent about one thing: Those who practice wellness every single day are the ones who build immunity. Sadly, most of us look at our health only when we fall ill. We neglect it otherwise and take our bodies for granted and most times abuse them. We begin exercising only if we realize we are putting on weight; we consume supplements only after the doctor tells us we are deficient. Why don't we care for our bodies every day? 'As a holistic health practitioner, I am for prevention. Take care every day,' he said.

And, as if he was reading my mind, he said, 'Why don't we write a book on the A to Z of daily wellness? Why don't we tell people the importance of being conscious about our daily wellness by eating the right food, doing the right exercise and getting adequate rest? Didn't COVID show us the urgent need to take charge of our health?'

I instantly agreed to write it and there began the journey of the book you are holding. Initially, the chapters had the A–Z of wellness, immunity and sleep. But knowing Dr Mathai and his passion for practising integrated medicine, we revisited the chapters along with the team at Penguin and felt the content was inadequate for people who wanted to take charge of their health. And that we must pump in more information.

We then added a separate chapter on the A–Z of common ailments, gut health, lifestyle modifications for wellness and the perils of consuming processed food. And it had to be wholesome and holistic advice from one of India's renowned health practitioners.

So every ailment or any advice on health had to be looked at from all forms of medicine—Ayurveda, Homeopathy and Naturopathy—before treating it. One form of medicine has never cured any disease is Dr Mathai's belief. Some ailments can be cured by a combination of medicines depending on their severity. Weak bones, says Dr Mathai, cannot be addressed with just antibiotics, they need to be cured with the right food and exercises. Good mental health is not just treated with tablets, but by practising yoga too, which is an ancient art.

Being a role model himself in practising daily wellness, which is a combination of the right food, exercise and rest, Dr Mathai's years of experience in treating patients from all over the world is all there in the book.

The book aims to tell readers the importance of being conscious about what you eat, how you work, how much you sleep and how all that contributes to how quickly you will heal when you fall sick. It probably is easier to practise daily wellness than spend all your life savings in hospitalization.

I would like to acknowledge the contribution of the doctors at SOUKYA, Dr Mathai's International Holistic Wellness Centre in Whitefield, Bengaluru, who helped in sharing the content of Dr Mathai's years of research in integrated medicine.

Seethalakshmi S.
Former city editor, *Times of India*, Bengaluru,
author of *Perils in Practice: Preventing Violence against Healthcare Professionals*, and
co-founder, Antardhwani, an independent think tank

Foreword

Our health and the health of the planet are one health.

Dr Mathai's ABC to Health, written with Seethalakshmi S., is a book everyone should read. It addresses the A to Z of common ailments and offers the A to Z of holistic approaches to wellness. The book is holistic in multiple dimensions. It offers approaches from diverse health traditions to even common ailments.

Dr Mathai also connects the health of the soil to our health, which helps us remember that the health of the planet and human health is one health. As the etymological root of the word 'health' reminds us, health is 'whole'; it creates 'wholesomeness' and the potential 'to heal'.

health (n.)

Old English *hælþ* 'wholeness, a being whole, sound or well', from Proto-Germanic **hailitho*, from PIE **kailo-* 'whole, uninjured, of good omen' (source also of Old

English *hal* 'hale, whole'; Old Norse *heill* 'healthy'; Old English *halig* and Old Norse *helge* 'holy, sacred'; Old English *hælan* 'to heal'.

Wholeness and the potential to heal arise from the self-organization and self-regulation of living organisms and living systems, through relationships of symbiosis and mutuality. Life is self-organized complexity and intelligence in constant evolution, interaction, change and emergence, and interconnectedness.

The ecological paradigm recognizes the self-organizing capacity, from microbes and cells to our bodies and Planet Earth. Self-organization is the ability to discriminate between necessary and harmful substances and flows. This is what makes life possible.

Planetary health and our health are one health, both in their interconnectedness of flows and the capacity for self-organization. Healthy relationships contribute to balance, dynamic stability or homeostasis and adaptive capacity and resilience.

One health is based on the principles of non-separability and potential, which are central to the quantum and ecological paradigm. Over the years, I see the health of ecosystems and organisms as a non-localized symphony in quantum coherence.

In this perspective, ecological degradation and disease are seen as an impairment in this capacity of self-organization, self-regulation, self-healing and the renewal of living systems.

Disease and sickness or dysbiosis have their roots in separation, pollution of the Earth's system, disruption of the Earth's ecological processes, and loss of biodiversity because of the domination of the mechanistic mind, which is blind to life in its complex self-organization.

One health begins with our consciousness that we are part of one interconnected living Earth, rich in biodiversity, and the potential for sickness and health lies in our diverse relationships that create, maintain and regenerate health.

One health transcends atomistic, fragmented thought. It recognizes our entanglement with other beings. We are interbeings. We are multispecies organisms. We are an ecological community. A complex self-organized, self-regulated ecosystem.

Our health and the health of the planet are one health. Our health is connected to the health of the soil of the seeds and plants we grow, the food we eat, the insects and microbes on which we depend, the water and the climate that sustain life.

Our health begins in healthy soils. Healthy soils are living systems. As Sir Albert Howard noted: '*The health of soil, plant, animal and man is one and indivisible.*'

The diversity of microbes in living soils produces the diversity of nutrients and phytochemicals that are necessary for health. That is why, as Dr Mathai writes, eating organic is a health imperative. Chemically grown food is not just decertifying the soil; it is producing nutritionally empty food.

A British meta-study covering more than 400 studies has found that organic foods can have up to

60 per cent more beneficial nutrients than chemically produced food.[1]

A Navdanya study comparing soils under chemical and organic conditions over twenty years showed a dramatic decline in soil nutrients under chemical farming and a significant increase in diverse nutrients under organic farming.[2]

Biodiversity is the source of health in the continuum of the web of life. Biodiversity makes healthy living soils, which produce healthy, nutritionally biodiversity-rich plants, which produce healthy biodiverse food that nourish the biodiversity of our gut, the basis of our health. The health of our gut microbiome is increasingly being recognized as the basis of our health. As Dr Mathai stresses in his book, health begins in the gut.

The biodiversity outside and the biodiversity within us are interrelated. The biodiversity in our soils, the biodiversity on our farms and plates, cultivates and nourishes the biodiversity in our gut microbiome. Our gut microbiome has 100 trillion micro-organisms and 100 species. There are 1,00,000 times more microbes in our gut than there are people on the planet.

There is an intimate connection between the biodiversity and health of soils, plants, our gut and our brain. Our gut is a microbiome that contains trillions of bacteria. To function in a healthy way, the gut microbiome needs a diverse diet, and a diverse diet needs diversity in our fields and gardens. A loss of diversity in our diet creates ill health.

The sophisticated understanding of nutrition in Ayurveda has shaped the diversity and healthy basis of India's traditional food cultures. Today, this rich dietary culture is threatened by the invasion of junk food and ultra-processed food.

When we destroy the biodiversity of our gut microbiome with chemically grown industrial food and ultra-processed food, chronic diseases like diabetes and cancer take on epidemic proportions.

How we grow our food and what we eat is the single biggest change each of us can make to regenerate the Earth by being conscious that health is holistic and begins with our food.

Begin your journey to health with the ABC to health and well-being by reading this book.

Vandana Shiva
Scholar, environmentalist and
food sovereignty advocate

of India's traditional food cultures. Today, this rich dietary culture is threatened by the invasion of junk food and ultra-processed food.

When we destroy the biodiversity of our gut microbiome with chemically grown industrial food and ultra processed food, chronic diseases like diabetes and cancer take on epidemic proportions.

How we grow our food and what we eat is the single biggest change each of us can make to regenerate the Earth by being conscious that health is one issue and begins with our food.

Begin your journey to health with the ABC to health and well being by reading this book.

Vandana Shiva
Scholar, environmentalist and
food sovereignty advocate

CHAPTER 1

The A–Z of Common Ailments

Underlying health conditions are medical conditions that interfere with daily life or activities and require medical attention and care.

Signs and symptoms are the results of a combination of genetic, physiological, environmental and behavioural factors. These signs and symptoms begin showing up due to unhealthy lifestyles and diets, and lack of physical activity. The signs are blood pressure (BP), increased blood glucose, elevated blood lipids and obesity. These are called metabolic risk factors that can eventually lead to cardiovascular and communicable diseases.

Here is the A–Z of common ailments that many of us have or have had during our lifetime. The treatment for each of these ailments varies from person to person and even from country to country. Dr Issac Mathai, who practises and promotes integrated medicine or the holistic approach to common ailments, believes it is crucial to choose the best form of treatment/medicine depending on the severity of the ailment. It is also vital to practise prevention when the ailment starts showing initial symptoms in your body.

Holistic Approach

Holistic medicine is a form of healing that considers the whole person's 'mind-body-soul' in the quest for optimal health and wellness. According to its philosophy, the primary goal of holistic medicine is to maintain a proper balance in life for optimal health.

Principles of Holistic Medicine

- All people have innate healing powers.
- The patient is a person, not a disease.
- Treatment involves fixing the cause of the condition, not just alleviating the symptoms.

Healing takes a team approach involving the patient and doctor and addresses all aspects of a person's life using traditional healthcare methods. Holistic health does incorporate complementary therapies that have been scientifically proven to work and, like alternative medicine, it focuses on wellness and prevention, rather than just treating diseases. In medicine, a cure refers to something that can completely eliminate a disease. Management is about lessening symptoms, preventing a disease from getting worse and relieving stress that may be associated with the illness.

Chronic diseases, by definition, cannot be cured—even with extensive lifestyle changes, medication and other treatments. However, chronic illnesses can be successfully managed and their symptoms can be reduced through holistic care.

Anxiety

Anxiety is a feeling of fear, dread and uneasiness. It might cause you to sweat, feel restless and tense, and have a rapid heartbeat. It can be a normal reaction to stress. For example, you might feel anxious when faced with a difficult problem at work, before taking an examination or before making an important decision.

Signs and Symptoms

1. Neurological, as headache, paraesthesia and vertigo
2. Digestive, as abdominal pain, nausea, diarrhoea, indigestion and dry mouth. Stress hormones released in an anxious state have an impact on bowel function and can manifest into physical symptoms
3. Respiratory, as shortness of breath or sighing breathing
4. Cardiac, in the form of palpitations, tachycardia or chest pain
5. Muscular, in the form of fatigue and tremors
6. Cutaneous, in the form of perspiration or itchy skin
7. Urogenital, as frequent urination, urinary urgency, dyspareunia or impotence and chronic pelvic pain syndrome

Types of Anxiety Disorders

Anxiety disorder: These are feelings that interfere with daily activities and may disrupt schedules with some lurking fear of something.

Panic disorder: This disorder occurs repeatedly and has physical symptoms too, such as shortness of breath, chest pain, etc.

Social anxiety disorder: In this, the person is apprehensive about interactions/gatherings with others as he/she fears humiliation, insults and being judged or embarrassed.

Specific phobia: In this, the person has a persistent fear of an activity, person or situation.

Causes

Anxiety disorders are like other forms of mental illnesses. They don't come from personal weakness, character flaws or problems with upbringing. A combination of factors plays a role:

- **Chemical imbalance:** Severe or long-lasting stress can change the chemical balance that controls your mood. Experiencing a lot of stress over a long period can lead to an anxiety disorder.
- **Environmental factors:** Experiencing a trauma might trigger an anxiety disorder, especially in someone who has inherited a higher risk to start with.
- **Heredity:** Anxiety disorders tend to run in families.

Holistic Approach

Ayurveda: Ayurvedic treatments such as Shirodhara, Thakradhara and Thalam, along with internal medications, help to calm down the mind and keep anxiety in control by bringing back the body–mind balance. Medicines that contain herbs such as ashwagandha, tagara and vacha are used in treating anxiety.

Naturopathy: Treatments such as spinal bath, mud bath and aroma oil massage.

Yoga: Trikonasana, Padahastasana, Marjaryasana, Balasana, Setu Bandhasana, Chandra Nadi Pranayama, relaxation and meditation techniques.

Follow-up: Hot bath with Epsom salts, hot foot bath.

Diet: Have soaked nuts (can be taken in the morning), flax seeds, pumpkin seeds (can be taken during breakfast, 1 tsp each), chamomile tea (can be taken in the evening or at bedtime), dark chocolate (small piece).

Homeopathy: Homeopathy is highly effective for treating different types of anxiety disorders. The prescription of homeopathic medicine is based on the principle of individualization. Homeopathic medicines reduce the frequency and intensity of panic attacks. Commonly prescribed medicines are Aconite, Arsenicum album, Argentum nitricum, Gelsemium, Kali phosphoricum and Calcarea carbonicum.

Backache

Backache is one of the most common medical complaints, particularly among adults. Backache usually refers to pain in your muscles, intervertebral joints, spinal nerves or sometimes, bone-on-bone pain. The type of pain you have can help your physician pinpoint the cause.

It may be classified as neck pain (cervical), middle back pain (thoracic), lower back pain (lumbar) or coccydynia (tailbone or sacral pain) based on the segment affected. The lumbar area is the most commonly affected area.

Causes

- ❖ Poor posture
- ❖ Lack of exercise resulting in stiffening of the spine and weak muscles
- ❖ Muscle strains or sprains
- ❖ An injury such as a pulled muscle (strain)
- ❖ Sometimes, medical conditions such as a slipped disc, sciatica (a trapped nerve) or ankylosing spondylitis
- ❖ Very rarely, back pain can be a sign of a serious problem such as a broken bone, cancer or infection

Top Tips

- ❖ **Keep your back mobile.** If you're in so much pain that you have to go to bed, that's fine, but try and get back on your feet as soon as possible.

- **Do not do any lifting.** If you do, you're likely to strain your back further.
- **Be careful while bending your back.** This puts a lot of strain on it, which can worsen your condition.

Holistic Approach

Ayurveda: Ayurvedic treatments such as Kati Vasti, Abhyanga, Patra Pinda Sweda, Vasti and Marmalepam, along with internal medications help relieve the pain and stiffness of the back by preventing the degeneration of bones and strengthening the muscles. Medicines such as Sahacharadi Kashayam, Maharasnadi Kashayam and Gulguluthikthakam Kashayam are used in the treatment of back pain.

Naturopathy: Treatments such as spinal bath, acupuncture, hot compress to back and infrared light.

Yoga: Setu Bandhasana, Shalabhasana, Supta matseyendrasana, Bhujangasana, relaxation and meditation techniques.

Follow-up: Massage with warm oil, hot fomentation, hot and cold compress alternatively, hot bath with Epsom salts.

Diet: Use of turmeric is good, chia seeds (1 tsp), olive oil (for cooking), sweet potato and carrot.

Homeopathy: There are several homeopathic medicines intended for back pain according to the cause of the pain and the situation of the person. If the pain is of chronic origin, constitutional medicine is given based on the holistic view of the case. Medicines such as Rhus tox, Bryonia, Kali carb, Hypericum, Ruta, Symphytum and Mag phos are helpful.

Constipation

Constipation occurs when bowel movements become less frequent and stool becomes difficult to pass. It happens most often due to changes in diet or routine, or due to inadequate intake of fibre. You should call your doctor if you have severe pain, blood in your stools or constipation that lasts longer than three weeks.

Other key features that usually define constipation include:

- Stools are dry and hard.
- Bowel movement is painful and stools are difficult to pass.
- You have a feeling that you have not fully emptied your bowels.

Causes

Constipation happens when your poo is hard and dry, making it difficult to pass. It's usually caused by:

- not eating enough fibre
- not drinking enough water
- not getting enough physical activity
- ignoring the urge to pass a stool when you need to
- being stressed or having a change in environment
- pregnancy
- overuse of laxatives
- certain medications, such as some painkillers or iron tablets

- medical conditions such as thyroid problems, Parkinson's disease, multiple sclerosis or depression
- problems with your digestive tract, such as irritable bowel syndrome, coeliac disease or diverticulitis

How does constipation happen?

Constipation happens because your colon absorbs too much water from waste (stool/poop), which dries out the stool making it hard in consistency and difficult to push out of the body. To back up a bit, as food normally moves through the digestive tract, nutrients are absorbed. The partially digested food (waste) that remains moves from the small intestine to the large intestine, also called the colon. The colon absorbs water from this waste, which creates a solid matter called stool. If you have constipation, the food **may move too slowly through the digestive tract.** This gives the colon more time—too much time—to absorb water from the waste. The stool thus becomes dry, hard and difficult to push out.

Holistic Approach

Ayurveda: Ayurvedic medications such as Triphala, Trivrit Lehyam, Gandharvahasta Thailam and Chiruvilwadi Kashayam, along with treatments such as Vasti and Abhyanga help to control constipation by subsiding the aggravated vata. These medicines, which are prepared naturally with ancient herbs, help to pacify the vata dosha or an aggravated vata and bring balance back to the body besides replenishing it.

Naturopathy: Treatments such as hot hip bath, enema, colon, abdominal massage and castor oil hot compress to the abdomen.

Yoga: Ardha kati asana, Ardhamatsyendrasana, Pavanmuktasana, Halasana and Vakrasana techniques.

Follow up: Hot compress to the abdomen and oil massage to the abdomen.

Diet: Use chia seeds (can be taken with water), boiled beetroot and carrot (before breakfast), buttermilk (lunch), papaya, oatmeal, bran flakes and apple (can be taken at breakfast).

Homeopathy: Homeopathic treatment of constipation is based on the cause leading to the development of constipation. Commonly indicated homeopathic medicines are Alumina, Nux vom, Silecia, Bryonia, Graphites, Plum met, Opium and Sulphur.

Depression

Depression is a mood disorder that causes a persistent feeling of sadness and loss of interest. Also called major depressive disorder or clinical depression, it affects how you feel, think and behave, and can lead to a variety of emotional and physical problems. You may have trouble doing normal day-to-day activities, and sometimes you may feel as if life isn't worth living.

Symptoms

Symptoms occur most of the day, nearly every day and may include:

- Feelings of sadness, tearfulness, emptiness or hopelessness
- Angry outbursts, irritability or frustration, even over small matters
- Loss of interest or pleasure in most or all normal activities, such as sex, hobbies or sports
- Sleep disturbances, including insomnia or sleeping too much
- Tiredness and lack of energy, so even small tasks take extra effort
- Reduced appetite and weight loss or increased cravings for food and weight gain
- Anxiety, agitation or restlessness
- Slowed thinking, speaking or body movements
- Feelings of worthlessness or guilt, fixating on past failures or self-blame
- Trouble thinking, concentrating, making decisions and remembering things

- Frequent or recurrent thoughts of death, suicidal thoughts, suicide attempts
- Unexplained physical problems, such as back pain or headaches

Causes

Experts believe depression is due to a combination of things:

Brain structure: The way certain nerve pathways or circuits in your brain send information may not work properly.

Genes: Scientists are studying certain genes that may make you more likely to get it. But even if you have them, you may not get depressed.

Life events: Something disturbing that happens to you may trigger depression. It may be the loss of someone close to you, a difficult relationship or a stressful situation.

Holistic Approach

Ayurveda: Medications with herbal supplements such as ashwagandha, brahmi, jatamamsi and yashtamadu can be taken along with guided breathing exercises for calming the mind.

Naturopathy: Treatments such as mud baths, circular jet, underwater massage and sauna bath.

Yoga: Utthita trikonasana, Balasana, Ardha chandrasana, Baddha konasana, Pranayama, relaxation and meditation techniques.

Follow-up: Hot foot bath and lavender oil massage to the back of the ear.

Diet: Brazil nuts (snacks), pumpkin seeds (1 tsp), tofu, pineapple, eggs (can be had for breakfast), chamomile tea (can be had in the evening or at bedtime).

Homeopathy: Homeopathic medicines get to the root cause of the disease and give a long-term solution for depression as we individualize the case and treat it holistically. After medication, we can notice changes in the feelings, behaviour and thoughts of patients. Medicines such as Ignatia, Nat mur, Sepia, Aur metallicum and Kali phos are helpful.

Diabetes

Diabetes is a disease that occurs when your blood glucose, also called blood sugar, is too high. Blood glucose is your main source of energy and comes from the food you eat. Insulin, a hormone made by the pancreas, helps glucose from food get into your cells to be used for energy. Sometimes your body doesn't make enough—or any—insulin or doesn't use insulin well. Glucose then stays in your blood and doesn't reach your cells. Over time, having too much glucose in your blood can cause health problems. Although diabetes has no cure, you can take steps to manage your diabetes and stay healthy.

Types

- **Type 1 diabetes** can develop at any age, but occurs most frequently in children and adolescents. When you have type 1 diabetes, your body produces very little or no insulin, which means that you need daily insulin injections to keep blood glucose levels under control.
- **Type 2 diabetes** is more common in adults and accounts for around 90 per cent of all diabetes cases. When you have type 2 diabetes, your body does not make good use of the insulin that it produces. The cornerstone of type 2 diabetes treatment is a healthy lifestyle, including increased physical activity and a healthy diet. However, over time, most people with type 2 diabetes will require oral

drugs and/or insulin to keep their blood glucose levels under control.

- Gestational diabetes (GDM) is a type of diabetes that consists of high blood glucose during pregnancy and is associated with complications for both mother and child.

Symptoms

Diabetes symptoms depend on how high your blood sugar is. Some people, especially if they have prediabetes or type 2 diabetes, may not have symptoms. In type 1 diabetes, symptoms tend to come on quickly and be more severe.

Some of the symptoms of type 1 diabetes and type 2 diabetes are:

- Feeling more thirsty than usual
- Urinating often
- Losing weight without trying
- Presence of ketones in the urine. Ketones are a by-product of the breakdown of muscle and fat that happens when there's not enough insulin available
- Feeling tired and weak
- Feeling irritable or having other mood changes
- Having blurry vision
- Having slow-healing sores
- Getting a lot of infections, such as gum, skin and vaginal infections

Complications

Heart disease, stroke, kidney disease, nerve damage, eye damage, digestion problems, erectile dysfunction, skin problems, infection and dental problems.

Holistic Approach

Ayurveda: Treatments such as Abhyanga, Choornasweda, Dhanyamlasweda and Vasti along with diet modification help to improve the metabolism. Also, medicines such as Nishakathakadi Kashayam helps control diabetes.

Naturopathy: Treatments such as gastro-hepatic pack, hip bath, acupuncture and massage.

Yoga: Ardhamatsyendrasana, Pavanmuktasana, Dhanurasana, Paschimottanasana, Bhujangasana, Pranayama, relaxation and meditation techniques.

Follow-up: Alternate hot and cold compress to the right and left side of the abdomen and hot foot bath.

Diet: Green vegetables, fenugreek seeds (morning or post meals), papaya, millets, Indian blackberry seeds powder (1 tsp can be taken in the morning with water).

Homeopathy: Homeopathy has a positive role in early diagnosed cases by correcting the constitution. The goal of the treatment is to prevent complications and improve the quality of life. There are some good homeopathic medicines to treat diabetes; some are Syzygium jambolanum, Helonias, Cephalandra, Uranium nitricum and Gymnema.

Eczema

Eczema is a condition in which patches of skin become inflamed, itchy, cracked and rough. Some types can also cause blisters. Atopic dermatitis (eczema) is a condition that causes dry, itchy and inflamed skin. It's common in young children but can occur at any age. Atopic dermatitis is long-lasting (chronic) and tends to flare sometimes. It can be irritating but it's not contagious. People with atopic dermatitis are at risk of developing food allergies, hay fever and asthma. Moisturizing regularly and following other skin care habits can relieve itching and prevent new outbreaks (flares). Treatment may also include medicated ointments or creams.

Symptoms

Atopic dermatitis (eczema) symptoms can appear anywhere on the body and vary widely from person to person. They may include:

- Dry, cracked skin
- Itchiness (pruritus)
- Rash on swollen skin that varies in colour depending on your skin colour
- Small, raised bumps on brown or black skin
- Oozing and crusting
- Thickened skin
- Darkening of the skin around the eyes
- Raw, sensitive skin from scratching

Where does eczema most commonly occur?

Eczema can show up anywhere on your skin. In teens and adults, it's typically found on your hands, neck, inner elbows, ankles, knees, feet and around your eyes.

Who is at risk of getting eczema?

Eczema (atopic dermatitis) usually begins in childhood, but anyone at any age can get it. You're at high risk if you are:

❖ Female
❖ Diagnosed with hay fever or asthma
❖ Part of a family with a history of dermatitis, hay fever or asthma

Causes

Eczema (atopic dermatitis) is caused by a combination of immune system activation, genetics, environmental triggers and stress.

Holistic Approach

Ayurveda: Abhyanga, Choornasweda, Lepanam, Khseeradhara, Navarakizhi and Virechana are done in the treatment of eczema. Also, medicines such as Haridrakhandam, Nimbadi Kashayam, Patoladi Kashayam and Thikthakam Kashayam are used in the treatment of eczema.

Naturopathy: Treatments such as atapa snana, ganji turmeric application, enema, steam bath with Epsom salts and underwater massage.

Yoga: Surya Namaskar, Pavanmuktasana, Dhanurasana, Anuloma viloma pranayama, Ujjai pranayama and meditation techniques.

Follow-up: Camphor and coconut oil application over affected parts, sun bath, turmeric and neem application.

Diet: Apple (can be taken in the morning), broccoli, spinach, kale, celery, flax seeds (1 tsp at lunch).

Homeopathy: There are many homeopathic medicines that can efficiently treat eczema by correcting the deranged immunity. Treatment varies from person to person based on age, sex, constitution, genetic predisposition, etc. Some of the commonly used medicines are Sulphur, Ars alb, Graphites, Sepia, Nat mur, Lycopodium, Petroleum and Psorinum.

Fatty Liver

The liver is the largest organ inside your body. It helps your body digest food, store energy and remove toxins. Fatty liver disease is a condition in which fat builds up in your liver

There are two main types:

- Non-alcoholic fatty liver disease (NAFLD)
- Alcoholic fatty liver disease (AFLD), also called alcoholic steatohepatitis

What is non-alcoholic fatty liver disease?

NAFLD is a type of fatty liver disease that is not related to heavy alcohol use. There are two kinds:

- **Simple fatty liver** in which you have fat in your liver but little or no inflammation or liver cell damage. Simple fatty liver typically does not get bad enough to cause liver damage or complications.
- **Non-alcoholic steatohepatitis** (NASH) is where you have inflammation and liver cell damage, as well as fat in your liver. Inflammation and liver cell damage can cause fibrosis, or scarring, of the liver. NASH may lead to cirrhosis or liver cancer.

What is alcoholic fatty liver disease?

Alcoholic fatty liver disease is due to heavy alcohol use. Your liver breaks down most of the alcohol you drink so that it can be removed from your body.

But the process of breaking it down can generate harmful substances. These substances can damage liver cells, promote inflammation and weaken your body's natural defences.

Symptoms

With AFLD and NAFLD, there are usually no symptoms. Some people may have signs such as tiredness or pain in the upper right side of the belly where the liver is.

If you have NASH or get cirrhosis, you may have symptoms such as:

- Swollen belly
- Enlarged blood vessels underneath your skin
- Larger-than-normal breasts in men
- Red palms
- Skin and eyes that appear yellowish, due to a condition called jaundice

Complications

- Fluid build-up in the abdomen (ascites)
- Swelling of veins in your oesophagus (oesophageal varices), which can rupture and bleed
- Confusion, drowsiness and slurred speech (hepatic encephalopathy)
- Liver cancer
- End-stage liver failure, which means the liver has stopped functioning

Between 5 and 12 per cent of people with NASH will progress to cirrhosis.

Holistic Approach

Ayurveda: Treatments such as Udwartana, Choornasweda, Dhanyamlasweda, Virechana and Vasti help to subside the aggravated Kapha and improve the fat metabolism. Medicines such as Varanadi Kashayam and Kanchanaraguggulu help in the treatment of fatty liver.

Naturopathy: Treatments such as hip bath, gastro-hepatic pack, steam bath, enema.

Yoga: Padmasana, Naukasana, Ardhamatsyendra asana, Vakrasana and Kapalbhati Pranayama.

Follow-up: Fruit diet and hot compress to the right side of the abdomen.

Diet: Papaya, sugarcane juice (can be taken at snack time), whole grain, fish, avocado, curd (avoid at night), flax seeds, green tea (evenings).

Homeopathy: Homeopathy is effective in treating fatty liver, finding a remedy through its holistic approach, individualization and symptom similarities. It's very effective in preventing relapses. Medicines such as Lycopodium, Chelidonium, Nat sulp, Nux vomica and Calcarea carb can be used.

Fibromyalgia

Fibromyalgia is a disorder characterized by widespread musculoskeletal pain accompanied by fatigue and sleep, memory and mood issues. Researchers believe that fibromyalgia amplifies painful sensations by affecting the way your brain and spinal cord process painful and non-painful signals.

Causes

The causes of fibromyalgia are unclear. Current research suggests involvement of the nervous system, particularly the central nervous system (brain and spinal cord). **Fibromyalgia is not from an autoimmune inflammation, joint or muscle disorder.** Fibromyalgia may run in families. There likely are certain genes that can make people more prone to getting fibromyalgia and the other health problems that can occur with it. Genes alone, though, do not cause fibromyalgia.

There is most often some triggering factor that sets off fibromyalgia. It may be spine problems, arthritis, injury or other types of physical stress. Emotional stress may also trigger this illness. The result is a change in the way the body talks with the spinal cord and brain. Levels of brain chemicals and proteins may change. More recently, fibromyalgia has been described as a central pain amplification disorder, meaning the volume of pain sensation in the brain is turned up too high.

Symptoms

Common fibromyalgia symptoms include:

- widespread pain
- joint and muscle stiffness after sleeping
- headaches
- irregular sleep patterns
- tingling and numbness in the hands and feet
- restless legs syndrome
- sensitivity to cold or heat
- difficulties with memory and concentration, known as 'fibro fog'
- fatigue
- irritable bowel syndrome (IBS)

The following may also occur:

- problems with vision
- nausea
- pelvic and urinary issues
- rapid weight gain
- dizziness
- cold or flu-like symptoms
- depression and anxiety
- post-traumatic stress disorder

Holistic Approach

Ayurveda: Treatments such as Choornasweda, Dhanyamlasweda, Dhanyamladhara, Abhyanga, Patra Potala Sweda, Lepam, Pichu and Vasti help to balance the aggravated doshas. Herbs such as triphala and guggulu preparations help control the inflammatory activity in the body.

Naturopathy: Treatments such as steam bath, massage therapy, underwater massage, spinal bath and Vichy shower.

Yoga: Setu Bandhasana, Shavasna, Sarvangasana, Uttanasna, Anuloma viloma pranayama, Pranayama, relaxation and meditation techniques.

Follow-ups: Hot bath with Epsom salts, sun bath and hot foot bath.

Diet: Nuts, flax seeds (1 tsp), tofu, pumpkin seeds (1 tsp), sesame seeds (1 tsp), dark chocolate (1 small piece), fenugreek seeds water (on an empty stomach).

Homeopathy: For fibromyalgia, we need to carefully assess both the physical and mental make-up of the patient before prescribing anything. A detailed case-taking, considering physical and emotional spheres, repertorization, individualization and a holistic approach, helps. Homeopathy offers several remedies for fibromyalgia, classified on the basis of discrete symptoms of the disease. Some medicines are Rhus tox, Ruta, Rhododendron, Arnica, Causticum, Kalmia and Mag phos.

Gastritis

Gastritis is a condition that inflames the stomach lining (the mucosa), causing belly pain, indigestion (dyspepsia), bloating and nausea. It can lead to other problems too. Gastritis can come on suddenly (acute) or gradually (chronic). Medications, treatments and dietary changes can reduce stomach acid and ease gastritis symptoms.

The stomach has a protective lining of mucus called the mucosa. This lining protects your stomach from the strong stomach acid that digests food. When something damages or weakens this protective lining, the mucosa becomes inflamed, causing gastritis. A type of bacteria called *Helicobacter pylori* is the most common bacterial cause of gastritis.

Causes

- Helicobacter pylori (H. pylori): A bacteria that lives in the mucous lining of the stomach; without treatment, the infection can lead to ulcers, and in some people, stomach cancer
- Bile reflux: A backflow of bile into the stomach from the bile tract (that connects to the liver and gall bladder)
- Infections caused by bacteria and viruses

Symptoms

Symptoms of gastritis vary among individuals, and in many people, there are no symptoms. However, the most common symptoms include:

- Nausea or recurrent upset stomach
- Abdominal bloating
- Abdominal pain
- Vomiting
- Indigestion
- Burning or gnawing feeling in the stomach between meals or at night
- Hiccups
- Loss of appetite
- Vomiting blood or coffee ground-like material
- Black, tarry stools

Types

- **Erosive (reactive):** Erosive gastritis causes both inflammation and erosion (wearing away) of the stomach lining. This condition is also known as reactive gastritis. Causes include alcohol, smoking, non-steroidal anti-inflammatory drugs (NSAIDs), corticosteroids, viral or bacterial infections and stress from illnesses or injuries.
- **Non-erosive:** Inflammation of the stomach lining without erosion or compromising the stomach lining.

Holistic Approach

Ayurveda: Ayurvedic treatments such as Khseeradhara, Nabeepooranam, Thakradhara and Abhyanga, and internal medication such as Avipathi Choorna and Gudoochyadi Kashayam help to improve the condition. Herbs such as guduchi and amla are also helpful.

Naturopathy: Treatments such as abdominal compress, hip bath, vamana and enema.

Yoga: Pavanmuktasana, Uttanpadasna, Bhujangasana, Dhanurasana and Sheetali Pranayama.

Follow-ups: Cold abdomen compress and cold water sipping.

Diet: Ash gourd juice (take it on an empty stomach), snake gourd, coriander juice (can be taken at snack time), jeera water (can be taken after meals), watermelon and chia seeds (can be taken with water).

Homeopathy: The aim of homeopathic medicine for gastritis is not only to treat gastritis but also to address its underlying cause and individual susceptibility. The selection of the medicine is based on individualization and totality of symptoms by a holistic approach. The main medicines used are Ars alb, Arg nit, Nux vom, China, Carbo veg, Lycopodium, Nat phos, Phos and Pulsatilla.

Headache

Nearly everyone has had headaches, and most of us have had them many times. A minor headache is little more than a nuisance that's relieved by an over-the-counter pain reliever, some food or coffee or a short rest. But if your headache is severe or unusual, you might worry about a stroke, a tumour or a blood clot. Fortunately, such problems are rare. Still, you should know when a headache needs urgent care and how to control the vast majority of headaches that are not threatening to your health.

Types

- Tension-type headache
- Migraine
- Exertional headache
- Medication-overuse headache
- Sinus headache
- Caffeine-related headache
- Head-injury headache
- Menstrual headache
- Hangover headache

Causes

Anything that stimulates the pain receptors in a person's head or neck can cause a headache, including:

- Stress
- Muscular tension
- Dental or jaw problems

- Infections
- Diet
- Eye problems
- Hormonal influences
- Medications
- Disorders of the ear, nose or throat
- Disorders of the nervous system
- Injury to the head, neck or spine
- High BP
- Poor posture—puts unnecessary strain on the muscles of the back and neck
- Hangover from abuse of alcohol or drugs
- Temperature—extremes of heat or cold
- Dehydration—affects BP
- Noise—especially loud noises
- Temporal arteritis—inflammation of the artery at the temple, most common in elderly people
- Arthritis
- Meningitis

Holistic Approach

Ayurveda: Treatments such as Shirodhara, Thakradhara, Thalam, Abhyanga, Nasyam and Vicharana Snehapanam are very beneficial for headaches. Herbs such as jeera and internal medications such as Pathyakshadhatryadi Kashayam are also beneficial.

Naturopathy: Treatments such as hot arm and foot bath, vamana, head massage, acupressure and acupuncture.

Yoga: Shashankasna, Balasana, Anuloma viloma pranayama, Pranayama, relaxation and meditation techniques, and Yoga nidra.

Follow-ups: Hot foot bath and steam inhalation.

Diet: Apple (breakfast), nuts, legumes, green leafy vegetables, pumpkin seeds, fennel water (can be taken before bed).

Homeopathy: Homeopathic medicines such as Belladonna, Bryonia, Sanguinaria, Iris versicolor and Spigelia are given according to the severity of the headache. This helps reduce the intensity and frequency of headaches. Homeopathic drugs work on similar principles: the success of the treatment lies in correctly identifying the medicine whose characteristics perfectly match the patient's set of symptoms.

Irritable Bowel Syndrome

Irritable bowel syndrome (IBS) is a group of symptoms that occur together, including repeated pain in your abdomen and changes in your bowel movements, which may be diarrhoea, constipation or both. With IBS, you have these symptoms without any visible signs of damage or disease in your digestive tract.

Types

- **IBS with constipation (IBS-C):** Most of your poop is hard and lumpy.
- **IBS with diarrhoea (IBS-D):** Most of your poop is loose and watery.
- **IBS with mixed bowel habits (IBS-M):** You have both hard and lumpy bowel movements and loose and watery movements on the same day.

Triggers

If you have IBS, you may have noticed that certain things trigger symptoms. Common triggers include some foods and medication. Emotional stress can also be a trigger. Some researchers suggest that IBS is the gut's response to life's stressors.

Causes

Researchers don't exactly know what causes IBS. They think a combination of factors can lead to IBS, including:

- ❖ **Dysmotility:** Problems with how your gastrointestinal (GI) tract muscles contract and move food through the tract.
- ❖ **Visceral hypersensitivity:** Extra-sensitive nerves in the GI tract.
- ❖ **Brain-gut dysfunction:** Miscommunication between nerves in the brain and the gut.

Symptoms

- ❖ Abdominal pain or cramps, usually in the lower half of the abdomen
- ❖ Bloating
- ❖ Bowel movements that are harder or looser than usual
- ❖ Diarrhoea, constipation or alternating between the two
- ❖ Excess gas
- ❖ Mucus in your poop (may look whitish)

Holistic Approach

Ayurveda: Ayurvedic treatments such as Khseeradhara, Nabeepooranam, Thakradhara and Thalam, and internal medication such as Indukantam Kashayam help to improve the condition.

Naturopathy and Yoga: Treatments such as hip bath, abdominal compress, peppermint oil massage to the abdomen and spinal bath.

Yoga: Ardha kati asana, Padhastasana, Ardha matsyendrasana, Yoga nidra, Anuloma viloma pranayama, relaxation and meditation techniques.

Follow-up: Alternate hot and cold compress to stomach.

Diet: Curd (avoid sour curd at night), tender coconut water, ash gourd juice (take on an empty stomach) and jeera water (before bedtime).

Homeopathy: IBS is usually cured with constitutional medicine. Treatment is based on symptoms and individualization, mainly focused on restoring the function of the gut, so that the root cause of IBS is taken care of. Lycopodium, Nux vom, Ars alb, Arg nitricum, Sulphur, Pulsatilla, etc., are some of the commonly prescribed medicines.

Joints Pain (Arthritis)

Arthritis is the swelling and tenderness of one or more joints. The main symptoms of arthritis are joint pain and stiffness, which typically worsen with age. The most common types of arthritis are osteoarthritis and rheumatoid arthritis.

Arthritis is most common in the following areas of the body:

- Feet
- Hands
- Hips
- Knees
- Lower back

Types

The most common types of arthritis include:

- **Osteoarthritis,** or 'wear and tear' arthritis, which develops when joint cartilage breaks down from repeated stress. It's the most common form of arthritis.
- **Ankylosing spondylitis,** or arthritis of the spine (usually your lower back).
- **Juvenile arthritis (JA),** a disorder where the immune system attacks the tissue around the joints. JA typically affects children of age sixteen or younger.
- **Gout,** a disease that causes hard crystals of uric acid to form in your joints.

- Psoriatic arthritis, joint inflammation that develops in people with psoriasis (an autoimmune disorder that causes skin irritation).
- Rheumatoid arthritis, a disease that causes the immune system to attack synovial membranes in your joints.

Causes

Different types of arthritis have different causes. For instance, gout is the result of too much uric acid in your body. But for other types of arthritis, the exact cause is unknown. You may develop arthritis if you:

- have a family history of arthritis
- have a job or play a sport that puts repeated stress on your joints
- have certain autoimmune diseases or viral infections

Symptoms

Different types of arthritis have different symptoms. They can be mild in some people and severe in others. Joint discomfort might come and go, or it could stay constant. Common symptoms include:

- Pain
- Redness
- Stiffness
- Swelling

- Tenderness
- Warmth

Holistic Approach

Ayurveda: Treatments such as Choornasweda, Vasti, Abhyanga, Lepam, Pichu and Pizhichil along with internal medications and rest can improve the condition by controlling the degenerative changes. Treatments such as Navarakizhi help to nourish the body also. Medicines prepared from Guggulu, Bala, Rasna and Guduchi are helpful.

Naturopathy: Treatments such as steam bath, massage therapy, underwater massage, infrared light, acupuncture and acupressure.

Yoga: Kapalbhati pranayama, Anuloma viloma and Yoga nidra.

Follow-up: Hot oil application to the painful area and a hot bath with Epsom salts.

Diet: Fenugreek water (empty stomach), garlic (3–4 raw pieces can be eaten), papaya and pineapple.

Homeopathy: Homeopathic treatment of joint pain aims to address the underlying cause of the condition along with reducing the pain and discomfort. Some of the medicines used for the treatment of joint pains are Arnica, Rhus tox, Bryonia, Calcarea phos, Ledum, Ruta, Colchicum and Pulsatilla.

Migraine

A migraine is a type of headache. It may occur with symptoms such as nausea, vomiting or sensitivity to light and sound. Migraine is a common neurological disease that causes a variety of symptoms, most notably a throbbing, pulsing headache on one side of your head. Your migraine will likely get worse with physical activity, lights, sounds or smells. It may last at least four hours or even days. Research shows that it's the sixth most disabling disease in the world.

Symptoms

Migraines are different for everyone. In many people, they happen in stages. These stages may include:

Prodrome

Hours or days before a headache, about 60 per cent of people who have migraines notice symptoms such as:

- Being sensitive to light, sound or smell
- Fatigue
- Food cravings or lack of appetite
- Mood changes
- Severe thirst
- Bloating
- Constipation or diarrhoea

Aura

These symptoms stem from your nervous system and often involve your vision. They usually start gradually, over a five to twenty-minute period and last less than an hour. You may:

- see black dots, wavy lines, flashes of light or things that aren't there (hallucinations)
- have tunnel vision
- not be able to see at all
- have tingling or numbness on one side of your body
- not be able to speak clearly
- have a heavy feeling in your arms and legs
- have ringing in your ears
- notice changes in smell, taste or touch

Causes

Migraine attacks may be triggered by any of the following:

- Caffeine withdrawal
- Changes in hormone levels during a woman's menstrual cycle or with the use of birth control pills
- Changes in sleep patterns, such as not getting enough sleep
- Drinking alcohol
- Exercise or other physical stress
- Loud noises or bright lights
- Missed meals

- Strong odours or perfumes
- Smoking or exposure to smoke
- Stress and anxiety

Holistic Approach

Ayurveda: Treatments such as Shirodhara, Thakradhara, Thalam, Abhyanga, Nasyam and Vicharana Snehapanam are very beneficial for headaches. Herbs such as jeera and internal medications such as Pathyakshadhatryadi Kashayam are beneficial.

Naturopathy: Treatments such as hot arm and foot bath, vamana, head massage, acupressure and acupuncture.

Yoga: Adho mukhasana, Balasna, Janushirsasana, Anuloma viloma, Yoga nidra, Brahmari pranayama, relaxation and meditation techniques.

Follow-ups: Hot foot bath, steam inhalation and desi ghee application in the nostrils during bedtime.

Diet: Apple (breakfast), nuts, legumes, green leafy vegetables, pumpkin seeds, fennel water (can be taken before bed), cumin, cardamom tea (mornings) and soaked raisins (empty stomach).

Homeopathy: Homeopathic medicine for migraine is taken into consideration not just by the symptoms, but also the cause. The individualistic symptoms and background of the attack are always unique to every person. Constitutional medicines help give a permanent cure for this condition. Some of the commonly used medicines are Belladonna, Gelsemium, Nat mur, Nux vomica, Sanguinaria, Spigelia, Iris versicolor and Ignatia.

Memory Loss

Memory loss is unusual forgetfulness. You may not be able to remember new events, recall one or more memories of the past, or both. The memory loss may be for a short time and then resolved (transient). Or, it may not go away and, depending on the cause, it can get worse over time. In severe cases, such memory impairment may interfere with daily living activities.

Causes

Normal ageing can cause some forgetfulness. It is normal to have some trouble learning new material or needing more time to remember it. But normal ageing does not lead to dramatic memory loss. Such memory loss is due to other diseases. Many areas of the brain help you create and retrieve memories. A problem in any of these areas can lead to memory loss.

Memory loss may result from a new injury to the brain, which is caused by or is present after:

- Brain tumour
- Cancer treatment, such as brain radiation, bone marrow transplant or chemotherapy
- Concussion or head trauma
- Not enough oxygen getting to the brain when your heart or breathing is stopped for too long
- Severe brain infection or infection around the brain
- Major surgery or severe illness, including brain surgery

- Transient global amnesia (sudden, temporary loss of memory) of unclear cause
- Transient ischaemic attack (TIA) or stroke
- Hydrocephalus (fluid collection in the brain)
- Multiple sclerosis
- Dementia
- Sometimes, memory loss occurs with mental health problems
- After a major traumatic or stressful event
- Bipolar disorder
- Depression or other mental health disorders, such as schizophrenia

Other causes of memory loss include:

- Alcohol or usc of prescription or illegal drugs
- Brain infections such as Lyme disease, syphilis or HIV/AIDS
- Overuse of medicines, such as barbiturates or hypnotics
- ECT (electroconvulsive therapy—most often short-term memory loss)
- Epilepsy that is not well controlled
- Illness that results in the loss of, or damage to, brain tissue or nerve cells, such as Parkinson's disease, Huntington's disease or multiple sclerosis
- Low levels of important nutrients or vitamins, such as low vitamin B1 or B12

Memory loss and ageing

Normal age-related memory loss does not cause a significant disruption in your daily life. For example, you might occasionally forget a person's name but recall it later in the day. You might misplace your glasses sometimes. Or maybe you need to make lists more often than in the past to remember appointments or tasks. These changes in memory are generally manageable and don't affect your ability to work, live independently or maintain a social life.

Memory loss and dementia

The word 'dementia' is an umbrella term used to describe a set of symptoms, including impairment in memory, reasoning, judgement, language and other thinking skills. Dementia usually begins gradually, worsens over time and impairs a person's abilities in work, social interactions and relationships.

Holistic Approach

Ayurveda: Ayurvedic treatments such as Shirodhara, Thakradhara, Ksheeradhara and Thalam along with internal medications help to improve concentration and memory by strengthening the nervous system. Internal medications that contain Brahmi, Shankapushpi, Mandookaparni and Jyotishmati are helpful in this condition.

Naturopathy: Spinal bath, acupressure, acupuncture and massage therapy.

Yoga: Tadasna, Vrakshasana, Yoga nidra, Trataka-meditation (flame meditation), Pranayama, relaxation and meditation techniques.

Follow-ups: A drop of castor oil application to the crown of the head at bedtime.

Diet: Sprouts (at breakfast or as a snack), brahmi juice (in the morning as well as evening), nuts, pumpkin seeds (1 tsp) and fatty fish.

Homeopathy: Homeopathy strengthens the immune system and also increases vitality. Homeopathy helps improve the symptoms of memory loss, poor concentration and learning difficulties in adults as well as in children. As there are no side effects, it won't lead to any drug dependency.

NEURALGIA

Neuralgia is pain in a nerve pathway. Generally, neuralgia isn't an illness in its own right, but a symptom of injury or a particular disorder. In many cases, the cause of the pain is not known. Older people are most susceptible, but people of any age can be affected. Almost everyone will experience mild neuralgia at some point, but these bouts are usually temporary and tend to ease by themselves within a few days. Some types of neuralgia are longer lasting, debilitating and so agonizing that a person's quality of life is severely reduced.

Trigeminal neuralgia, a condition that usually affects one side of the face only, is said to be one of the most painful medical conditions. Neuralgia can be managed with medication and physical therapy. Surgery is an option in some resistant cases.

The area may be excruciatingly sensitive to touch, and any pressure is felt as pain.

Symptoms

- Localized pain
- The pain can be sharp or burning, depending on the affected nerve
- The affected area is still functional
- The muscles may spasm

Nerve inflammation can trigger neuralgia

- **Shingles:** Inflammation of a nerve, caused by infection with the herpes virus. This common type of neuralgia is known as post-herpetic neuralgia. The pain may remain long after the shingles rash has disappeared, particularly in areas of the face.

- **Infection:** The nerve can be irritated by nearby infection, such as a tooth abscess.
- **Pressure or injury:** Broken bones, slipped vertebral discs (sciatica) or certain tumours can press and irritate a nerve.
- **Syphilis:** In its advanced stages, this sexually transmitted disease affects the functioning of the nervous system.

Holistic Approach

Ayurveda: Ayurvedic therapies such as Abhyanga, Patra Pinda Sweda, Pizhichil, Navarakizhi and Vasti help to relieve the neurological deficits. Treatments also help to strengthen the neurons. Medicines that help to reduce vata such as Ksheerabala and Dashamoola are very effective for this condition.

Naturopathy: Treatments such as massage therapy, steam bath, underwater massage and mud bath.

Yoga: Pachimotanasana, Vakrasana, Gomukasana, Pranayama, Yoga nidra, relaxation and meditation techniques.

Follow-ups: Hot bath with Epsom salts.

Diet: Sprouts (at breakfast or as a snack), egg, flax seeds (1 tsp), broccoli, spinach and nuts.

Homeopathy: A homeopathic holistic approach helps the sick individual to maintain a balance at mental, emotional and physical levels. The selection of neuralgic medicine depends on individualization, considering the physical and emotional make-up of the patient. Some common medicines given are Hypericum, Agaricus, Causticum, Zincum met, Cup met, Kalmia and Gelsemium.

Osteoarthritis

Osteoarthritis (OA) is a very common condition that can affect any joint in the body. It's most likely to affect the joints that bear most of our weight, such as the knees and feet. Joints that we use a lot in everyday life, such as the joints of the hand, are also commonly affected.

Causes

Factors that may contribute to the development of OA include:

- **Age:** The risk of developing OA increases with age and symptoms generally, but not always, appear in people over fifty.
- **Joint injury:** A bone fracture or cartilage or ligament tear can lead to OA, sometimes more quickly than in cases where there is not an obvious injury.
- **Overuse:** Using the same joints over and over in a job or sport can result in OA.
- **Obesity:** Excess weight adds stress and pressure on a joint, plus fat cells promote inflammation.
- **Musculoskeletal abnormalities:** Malalignment of bone or joint structures can contribute to the faster development of OA.
- **Weak muscles:** If muscles do not provide adequate joint support, poor alignment can result, which can lead to OA.
- **Genetics:** People with family members who have OA are more likely to develop it.

- **Gender:** Women are more likely to develop OA than men.
- **Environmental factors:** Modifiable environmental risk factors include things such as someone's occupation, level of physical activity, quadriceps strength, presence or absence of prior joint injury, obesity, diet, sex hormones and bone density.

Symptoms

Symptoms tend to build over time rather than show up suddenly. They include:

- Pain or aching in a joint during activity, after long activity or at the end of the day
- Joint stiffness that usually occurs first thing in the morning or after resting
- Limited range of motion that may go away after movement
- Clicking or popping sound when a joint bends
- Swelling around a joint
- Muscle weakness around the joint
- Joint instability or buckling (as when a knee gives out)

OA may affect different parts of the body in different ways.

- **Hips:** Pain in the groin area or buttocks and sometimes on the inside of the knee or thigh.
- **Knees:** A grating or scraping feeling when moving the knee.

- **Fingers:** Bony growths (spurs) at the edge of joints can cause fingers to become swollen, tender and red, sometimes with pain at the base of the thumb.
- **Feet:** Pain and tenderness in the big toe, with possible swelling in the ankles or toes.

Who is affected by osteoarthritis?

Approximately 80 per cent of older adults, aged fifty-five years and older, have evidence of osteoarthritis on X-ray. Of these, an estimated 60 per cent experience symptoms. It is estimated that 240 million adults worldwide have symptomatic osteoarthritis, including more than 30 million US adults. Post-menopausal women have an increased incidence of knee osteoarthritis as compared to men.

Holistic Approach

Ayurveda: Treatments such as Choornasweda, Vasti, Abhyanga, Lepam, Pichu and Pizhichil along with internal medications and rest can improve the condition by controlling the degenerative changes. Treatments such as Navarakizhi help to nourish the body also. Medicines such as Rasnadi Kashayam and Yogarajaguggulu Vatika are helpful.

Naturopathy: Treatments such as massage therapy, steam bath, sauna bath, underwater massage, acupuncture and infra-red.

Yoga: Kapalbhati pranayama, Anuloma viloma and Yoga nidra.

Follow-up: Hot oil application to the painful area and hot bath with Epsom salts.

Diet: Fenugreek water (empty stomach), garlic (3–4 pieces eaten raw), papaya and pineapple.

Homeopathy: In OA, the aim of the treatment is to manage the pain, prevent further damage to joints and improve mobility. Rhus tox, Bryonia, Colchicum, Pulsatilla, Cal carb, Kali carb, Gnaphallium, Eupatorium and Rhododendron are some of the medicines.

Overweight

A person whose weight is higher than what is considered to be the normal weight for a given height is described as being overweight or having obesity. Body mass index (BMI) is a simple index of weight for height that is commonly used to classify overweight and obesity in adults. It is defined as a person's weight in kilograms divided by the square of his height in metres (kg/m^2).

Types

- **Class I obesity:** BMI 30 to <35 kg/m^2
- **Class II obesity:** BMI 35 to <40 kg/m^2
- **Class III obesity:** BMI 40+ kg/m^2

How can obesity affect your health?

Obesity can help explain some conditions you may have, such as:

- High BP
- Heart disease and stroke
- Type 2 diabetes
- High cholesterol
- Joint problems caused by extra weight
- Trouble breathing, including sleep apnea, in which you briefly stop breathing while you're asleep
- Gallstones

Causes

The fundamental cause of obesity and overweight is an energy imbalance between calories consumed and calories expended. Globally, there has been:

- An increased intake of energy-dense foods that are high in fat and sugars; and
- An increase in physical inactivity due to the increasingly sedentary nature of many forms of work, changing modes of transportation and increasing urbanization

Changes in dietary and physical activity patterns are often the result of environmental and societal changes associated with development and the lack of supportive policies in sectors such as health, agriculture, transport, urban planning, environment, food processing, distribution, marketing and education.

Holistic Approach

Ayurveda: Treatments such as Snehapanam, Udwartana, Choornasweda, Dhanyamlasweda, Virechana and Lekhana Vasti help to subside the aggravated Kapha and improve fat metabolism. Medicines such as Varanadi Kashayam, Kanchanaraguggulu and Gugguluthikthaka Kashayam help lose weight.

Naturopathy: Treatments such as massage therapy, diet therapy, steam bath, circular jet and sauna bath.

Yoga: Surya Namaskar, Padhastasana, Trikonasana, Halasana, Sarvangasana and Shashankasana.

Follow-ups: Cold water shower and diet therapy.

Diet: Fibre-rich diet, oatmeal, papaya, watermelon, lemon honey water (on an empty stomach in the morning), sprouts (at breakfast as well as a snack).

Homeopathy: The selection of homeopathic medicines is based on the cause of the condition. Medicines work by increasing the metabolic rate of the body and have to be accompanied by exercise and a balanced diet. The holistic approach is the best way to treat overweight. Calcarea carb, Phytolacca, Graphites and Baryta carb are helpful in treating overweight.

Postmenopausal Syndrome

Postmenopause is the time after you've been without a menstrual period for twelve months. During this stage, women may experience symptoms such as hot flashes and mood swings. People in postmenopause are at increased risk for osteoporosis and heart diseases. Medication treatments or healthy lifestyle changes may reduce the risk of these conditions.

At this stage in life, your reproductive years are behind you and you're no longer ovulating (releasing eggs). The menopausal symptoms you've experienced in the past may become milder or go away completely. However, some people continue to experience menopausal symptoms for a decade or longer after menopause.

There are three stages of menopause: perimenopause, menopause and postmenopause.

- **Perimenopause** is the time leading up to menopause. It describes a time when hormones start to decline and menstrual cycles become erratic and irregular. You may start to experience the side effects of menopause, such as hot flashes or vaginal dryness.
- **Menopause** occurs when you've stopped producing the hormones that cause your menstrual period and have gone without a period for twelve months in a row. Once this has occurred, you enter postmenopause.
- **Postmenopause** is the time after menopause has occurred. Once this happens, you're in

postmenopause for the rest of your life. At this stage, your risk for osteoporosis and heart diseases increases.

Hormonal changes happen after menopause

Your ovaries are making very little of both oestrogen and progesterone by the time you're in postmenopause. Some people still experience side effects from low hormone levels.

Symptoms

Most people in postmenopause feel lingering symptoms from menopause, but these symptoms are less intense. In some cases, they almost disappear. Lingering symptoms are caused by low levels of reproductive hormones.

People in postmenopause can feel symptoms such as:

- ❖ Hot flashes and night sweats
- ❖ Vaginal dryness and sexual discomfort
- ❖ Depression
- ❖ Changes in sex drive
- ❖ Insomnia
- ❖ Dry skin
- ❖ Weight changes
- ❖ Hair loss
- ❖ Urinary incontinence

Holistic Approach

Ayurveda: Treatments such as Shirodhara, Abhyanga, Virechana and Pizhichil Vasti help to set right the hormonal imbalance. Guduchyadi Kashayam is helpful in controlling hot flashes.

Naturopathy: Treatments such as massage therapy, circular jet, Vichy shower, mud bath and sauna bath.

Yoga: Padhastasna, Matsyasana, Balasana, Makrasana, Yoga nidra, Pranayama, relaxation and meditation techniques.

Follow-up: Hot bath with Epsom salts and hot foot bath.

Diet: Nuts, flax seeds, tofu, pumpkin seeds (1 tsp), sesame seeds (1 tsp), dark chocolate (1 small piece), fenugreek seeds water (empty stomach).

Homeopathy: The treatment of postmenopausal ailments is holistic and one has to find the constitutional medicine based on the totality of symptoms. Homeopathic treatment works on balancing the hormones and improving energy. Some medicines used for postmenopausal ailments are Lachesis, Sepia, Calcarea carb, Pulsatilla, Cimcifuga and Graphites.

Quit Smoking

It's never too late to quit smoking. Various research studies have proved that nicotine (the main ingredient of tobacco products) causes cancer and other lung/ heart and respiratory diseases.

Nicotine Replacement Therapy

Nicotine in cigarettes can lead to unpleasant withdrawal symptoms when smokers try to quit. Nicotine Replacement Therapy (NRT) provides a low level of nicotine without the other poisonous chemicals in tobacco smoke.

It can help ease some of the symptoms of nicotine withdrawal, which include:

- Intense cravings
- Nausea
- Tingling of hands and feet
- Insomnia
- Mood swings
- Difficulty in concentrating

NRT is available as:

- Gum
- Patches
- Sprays
- Inhalers
- Lozenges

Patches are available from a pharmacy without a prescription. They slowly release nicotine, which the body absorbs through the skin. Gradually, the amount of nicotine reduces as the person switches to lower-dose patches. Eventually, they will no longer crave the substance. Some people wear their patches continually and have a steady dose of nicotine over twenty-four hours, while others remove them at night. A doctor can advise on the best option. Inhalers, gum, lozenges and sprays work quickly, but their effects last only for a short time. They can help relieve intense cravings, while patches provide a daily dose.

Holistic Approach

Ayurveda: Ayurvedic treatments such as Snehapanam, Shirodhara, Thakradhara, Nasyam, Virechana and Thalam along with internal medications such as Kalyanakam Kashayam and Manasamitra Vati help to calm down the mind and reduce the craving for tobacco.

Naturopathy: Treatments such as sauna bath, massage therapy and reflexology.

Yoga: Bhujangasana, Sarvangasana, Halasana Kapalbhati, Pranayama, Yoga nidra, relaxation and meditation techniques.

Follow-up: Diet therapy, yoga therapy and hot foot bath.

Diet: Citrus fruits, jeera water (empty stomach), ginseng tea (evening) and ginger-mint water tea (at bedtime).

Homeopathy: Homeopathy has remedies that help reduce nicotine cravings. It offers a safe and reliable method for treatment. The holistic approach is the better way as we look at individual symptoms to correlate the best constitutional remedy. Some medicines to stop smoking are Tabacum, Nux vom, Lobelia, Caladium and Daphne indica.

Restless Legs Syndrome

Restless legs syndrome (RLS), also called Willis-Ekbom Disease, causes unpleasant or uncomfortable sensations in the legs and an irresistible urge to move them. Symptoms commonly occur in the late afternoon or evening hours, and are often most severe at night when a person is resting, such as sitting or lying in bed. They may also occur when someone is inactive and sitting for extended periods (for example, when taking a trip by plane or watching a movie). Since symptoms can increase in severity during the night; it could become difficult to fall asleep or return to sleep after waking up.

Moving the legs or walking typically relieves the discomfort but the sensations often recur once the movement stops. RLS is classified as a sleep disorder since the symptoms are triggered by resting and attempting to sleep, and as a movement disorder, since people are forced to move their legs in order to relieve symptoms. It is, however, best characterized as a neurological sensory disorder with symptoms that are produced from within the brain itself.

Simple self-care steps and lifestyle changes may help relieve symptoms. Medications also help many people with RLS.

Symptoms

The chief symptom is an urge to move the legs. Common accompanying characteristics of RLS include:

- ❖ **Sensations that begin while resting:** The sensation typically begins after you've been lying down or sitting for an extended time, such as in a car, airplane or movie theatre.
- ❖ **Relief with movement:** The sensation of RLS lessens with movement, such as stretching, jiggling the legs, pacing or walking.
- ❖ **Worsening of symptoms in the evening:** Symptoms occur mainly at night.
- ❖ **Night-time leg twitching:** RLS may be associated with another, more common condition called periodic limb movement of sleep, which causes the legs to twitch and kick, possibly throughout the night while you sleep.

The sensations, which generally occur within the limb rather than on the skin, are described as:

- ❖ Crawling
- ❖ Creeping
- ❖ Pulling
- ❖ Throbbing
- ❖ Aching
- ❖ Itching
- ❖ Electric

Sometimes, the sensations are difficult to explain. People with RLS usually don't describe the condition as a muscle cramp or numbness. They do, however, consistently describe the desire to move the legs.

Holistic Approach

Ayurveda: Ayurvedic therapies such as Padabyanga, Patra Pinda Sweda, Pizhichil and Vasti help to relax the excited nerves and reduce RLS. Medicines containing Dashamoola, Sahachara and Bala are good for treating this condition.

Naturopathy: Treatments such as massage therapy, acupuncture, reflexology and underwater massage.

Yoga: Bhadakonasana, Vipreetkarani, Yoga nidra, Anuloma viloma, Brahmari, Pranayama, relaxation and meditation techniques.

Follow-ups: Hot foot bath.

Diet: Green leafy vegetables, nuts, flax seeds (1 tsp), lentils and sprouts (can be taken at breakfast as well as a snack).

Homeopathy: Homeopathic treatment offers complete recovery from RLS. Medicines help in relaxing the nervous system, thus controlling the uncomfortable sensation in the legs. Rhus tox, Zincum met, Aconite, Causticum, Ignatia, Ferr met, Kali phos and Tarentula are some medicines that can be considered.

Sciatica

Sciatica is a common type of pain affecting the sciatic nerve, a large nerve extending from your lower back down the back of each leg. Sciatica pain is caused by irritation, inflammation, pinching or compression of a nerve in the lower back. The most common cause is a herniated or slipped disk that causes pressure on the nerve root. Most people with sciatica get better on their own with time and self-care treatments.

What does sciatica feel like?

The symptoms of sciatica are commonly felt along the path of the large sciatic nerve. Sciatica is often characterized by one or more of the following features:

- **Pain:** Sciatica pain is typically felt like a constant burning sensation or a shooting pain starting in the lower back or buttock and radiating down the front or back of the thigh and leg and/or feet.
- **Numbness:** Sciatica pain may be accompanied by numbness in the back of the leg. Sometimes, tingling and/or weakness may also be present.
- **One-sided symptoms:** Sciatica typically affects one leg. The condition often results in a feeling of heaviness in the affected leg.[1] Rarely, both legs may be affected together.
- **Posture-induced symptoms:** Sciatica symptoms may feel worse while sitting, trying to stand up, bending the spine forward, twisting the spine, lying

down, and/or while coughing. The symptoms may be relieved by walking or applying a heat pack over the rear pelvic region.

Sciatica is the symptom of an underlying medical condition. Common medical conditions that may cause sciatica include:

- A herniated lumbar disc
- Lumbar spinal stenosis
- Lumbar degenerative disc disease, general degenerative changes in vertebrae or discs
- Spondylolisthesis
- Muscle spasm and/or inflammation of the lumbar and/or pelvic muscles
- Sacroiliac joint dysfunction

Holistic Approach

Ayurveda: Ayurvedic therapies such as Abhyanga, Kativasti, Patra Pinda Sweda, Pizhichil and Navarakizhi help to relieve the inflammatory changes and the radiating pain by releasing the sciatic nerve root compression. Treatments also help to nourish and strengthen the supportive tissues holding the spine.

Naturopathy: Treatments such as infra-red, acupuncture, spinal bath, reflexology, steam bath and massage therapy.

Yoga: Padhastasana, Janushirsana, Setu Bandhasana, Bhujangasana, Pranayama, relaxation and meditation techniques.

Follow-up: Hot foot bath, hot oil application and yoga therapy.

Diet: Fenugreek water (empty stomach), garlic (3–4 pieces eaten raw) and pineapple.

Homeopathy: Homeopathy can cure acute and chronic sciatic pain with a holistic approach. Homeopathic medicines not only rectify sciatic pain but also help in strengthening a patient's constitution, so that the disease is cured of its root and there are no further recurrences. Some medicines used are Colocynthis, Mag phos, Rhus tox, Bryonia, Hypericum, Gnaphallium, Ruta, Colchicum and Calcarea carb.

Tremors

A tremor is an involuntary, somewhat rhythmic, muscle contraction and relaxation involving oscillations or twitching movements of one or more body parts. It is the most common of all involuntary movements and can affect the hands, arms, eyes, face, head, vocal folds, trunk and legs. Most tremors occur in the hands. In some people, a tremor is a symptom of another neurological disorder. A very common tremor is teeth chattering, usually induced by cold temperatures or by fear.

- Symptoms begin gradually, usually more prominently on one side of the body
- They worsen with movement
- They usually occur in the hands first, affecting one hand or both hands
- They can include a 'yes-yes' or 'no-no' motion of the head
- They may be aggravated by emotional stress, fatigue, caffeine or temperature extremes

What is essential tremor?

Essential tremor is a movement disorder that causes parts of your body to shake. This kind of shaking isn't controllable, and you can't keep yourself from doing it. Essential tremor usually affects your hands and arms but can also affect your head, voice and other body parts.

In its advanced stages, this condition can severely disrupt some of the most basic tasks and parts of life, such as eating, drinking and dressing yourself. Many people also struggle with feelings of embarrassment or anxiety about the symptoms of this condition.

Holistic Approach

Ayurveda: Treatments such as Shirodhara, Shirovasti, Thalam Pizhichil and Vasti help to strengthen the nervous system by subsiding the vitiated vata. Medicines containing ashwagandha, bala and kapikachu are good for treating this condition.

Naturopathy: Treatments such as massage therapy, acupuncture, reflexology and underwater massage.

Yoga: Bhadakonasana, Padauthanasna, Anuloma viloma, Brahmari, Yoga nidra, Pranayama, relaxation and meditation techniques.

Follow-up: Bath with Epsom salts.

Diet: Green leafy vegetables, soaked nuts (in the morning), flax seeds (1 tsp), lentils and sprouts (morning).

Homeopathy: Homeopathy helps the patient initially by reducing the intensity and frequency of symptoms and slowly bringing about a cure. Constitutional medicine always works. Some medicines for tremors are Agaricus, Gelsemium, Nux moschata, Zin met, Phos, Silecia, Plum met and Lachesis.

Ulcerative Colitis

Ulcerative colitis is an inflammatory bowel disease. It causes irritation, inflammation and ulcers in the lining of your large intestine (also called your colon). Inflammation in ulcerative colitis starts in the rectum and may spread to the colon. Symptoms may be constant or may come and go. They include diarrhoea, weight loss, abdominal cramping, anaemia and blood or pus in bowel movements. There's no cure for ulcerative colitis. Medications and treatments can help calm the inflammation.

Causes

Researchers think the cause of ulcerative colitis is complex and involves many factors. They think it's probably the result of an overactive immune response. The immune system's job is to protect the body from germs and other dangerous substances. But sometimes, your immune system mistakenly attacks your body, which causes inflammation and tissue damage. Stress and certain foods can trigger symptoms, but they do not cause ulcerative colitis. Ulcerative colitis may affect any age group. There are peaks between ages fifteen and thirty, and then again at ages fifty to seventy. The disease begins in the rectal area. It may stay in the rectum or spread to higher areas of the large intestine. However, the disease does not skip areas. It may involve the entire large intestine over time.

Symptoms

Ulcerative colitis symptoms often get worse over time. In the beginning, you may notice:

- Diarrhoea or urgent bowel movements
- Abdominal (belly) cramping
- Tiredness
- Nausea
- Weight loss
- Anaemia (reduced number of red blood cells)

Later you may also have:

- Blood, mucus or pus in bowel movements
- Severe cramping
- Fever
- Skin rashes
- Mouth sores
- Joint pain
- Red, painful eyes
- Liver disease
- Loss of fluids and nutrients

Holistic Approach

Ayurveda: Ayurvedic treatments such as Khseeradhara, Nabeepooranam and Thakradhara and internal medication such as Kalashakaadi Kashayam help to improve the condition.

Naturopathy: Treatments such as abdominal compress, underwater massage, hip bath and massage therapy.

Yoga: Sarvangasana, Pavanmuktasana, Anuloma viloma, Shetali pranayama, Yoga nidra, Pranayama, relaxation and meditation techniques.

Follow-up: Diet therapy and cold pack to stomach.

Diet: Fennel water (empty stomach), curds (avoid sour curds and at night too), boiled rice, pumpkin (soup form), ash gourd juice (twice a day), and spicy foods should be avoided.

Homeopathy: Homeopathy is extremely effective in treating ulcerative colitis. Homeopathic medicines address the underlying pathology and help in correcting the immune system, which is responsible for ulcer formation in the intestinal tract. The holistic or constitutional approach yields positive results. Some of the remedies for ulcerative colitis include Ars alb, Mercor, Mer sol, Acid nitricum and Argentum nitricum.

Viral Fever

Viral fever is an umbrella term for a group of viral infections that affect the body, which is characterized by high fever, burning in the eyes, headaches, body aches and sometimes nausea and vomiting. Viral fever is common among children and older people as their immunity is lower. The fever by itself is not an illness; it is a symptom of an underlying cause, which is a viral infection. A viral infection can occur in any part of the body, intestines, lungs, air passages, etc. The fever will occur as a result of the infection. The high fever is usually a sign of the immune system of the body fighting against the intruding viruses and 'burning them off'. A body temperature of about 98.6°F (37°C) is normal, and anything higher than 100.4°F is considered a fever. When you have the flu or cold, your body temperature spikes due to viral infection.

Symptoms

- Both joint and muscle aches
- Headache
- Fatigue
- Sore throat
- Runny nose
- An increase in body temperature
- Dehydration
- Frequent chills
- Redness of eyes
- Skin rashes
- Appetite loss

Causes

- ❖ Viruses are a very small type of infectious agent. They invade and multiply throughout your body's cells.
- ❖ Viral sickness can be caused due to various viruses, including cold and flu viruses.
- ❖ Food and drinks may be contaminated with deadly viruses. Swallowing contaminated food can lead to some viral infections such as norovirus and enteroviruses.
- ❖ Viruses carried by insects or animals can cause viral infections such as fever and rabies.
- ❖ Exchanging bodily fluids with a person who has a viral infection can cause hepatitis B and HIV.
- ❖ Due to low immunity, babies and children have a high risk of getting viral infections.
- ❖ Elderly people are more prone to viral infections as they have very weak immune systems.
- ❖ Getting in contact with the contaminated area can lead to viral infections.

Holistic Approach

Ayurveda: Internal medications such as Sudarshana Vati, Dashamoola Katutraya Kashayam and Amrutottara Kashayam along with rest help the body fight against viral infections by improving immunity.

Naturopathy: Treatments such as wet sheet pack, sponge bath, arm and foot bath and fasting therapy.

Yoga: Anuloma viloma, Brahmari pranayama, Shavasana, Pranayama, relaxation and meditation techniques.

Follow-up: Hot foot bath and cold compress to the forehead.

Diet: Vegetable soup, ginger tea (morning), watermelon, apple, pineapple, kiwi, poultry broths and coconut water (as a snack).

Homeopathy: The selection of homeopathic medicine for viral fever is based on the theory of individualization and symptom similarity using the holistic approach. There are several proven medicines available for viral fever that we need to select based on the cause, sensation and modalities of the complaint. The aim of the homeopathic treatment is not only to treat the fever but also to address the underlying cause and individual susceptibility. Some medicines for viral fever are Belladonna, Rhus tox, Bryonia, Nux vom, Eupatorium, Pulsatilla and Pyrogenum.

Warts

These small, non-cancerous growths appear when your skin is infected with one of the many viruses of the human papillomavirus (HPV) family. The virus triggers extra cell growth, which makes the outer layer of the skin thick and hard in that spot. Common warts are small, grainy skin growths that occur most often on your fingers or hands. Rough to the touch, common warts also often feature a pattern of tiny black dots, which are small, clotted blood vessels.

Common warts are caused by a virus and are transmitted by touch. It can take a wart as long as two to six months to develop after your skin has been exposed to the virus. Common warts are usually harmless and eventually disappear on their own. But many people choose to remove them because they find them bothersome or embarrassing.

Types of warts include:

Common warts: Usually found on fingers, hands, knees and elbows. A common wart is a small, hard bump that's dome-shaped and usually greyish-brown. It has a rough surface that may look like the head of a cauliflower, with black dots inside.

Flat warts: These are about the size of a pinhead, are smoother than other kinds of warts and have flat tops. Flat warts may be pink, light brown or yellow. Most kids who get flat warts have them on their faces, but they can grow anywhere and can appear in clusters.

Plantar warts: Found on the bottom of the foot, plantar warts can be very uncomfortable, and feel as if you're walking on a small stone.

Filiform warts: These have a finger-like shape, are usually flesh-coloured, and often grow on or around the mouth, eyes or nose.

Symptoms

Common warts usually occur on your fingers or hands and may be:

- Small, fleshy, grainy bumps
- Rough to touch
- Sprinkled with black pinpoints, which are small, clotted blood vessels

Holistic Approach

Ayurveda: Local applications prepared out of herbs such as arka, shunti, jambeera and apamarga are found to be effective in managing warts.

Naturopathy: Treatments such as arm and foot bath, salt glow massage and underwater massage.

Yoga: Balasana, Kapalbhati pranayama, Anuloma viloma pranayama, Yoga nidra, Pranayama, relaxation and meditation techniques.

Follow-up: Epsom salts bath.

Diet: Sprouts (for breakfast), curds (avoid at night), green vegetables, tomatoes, berries and citrus fruits (as a snack).

Homeopathy: When using homeopathic remedies for warts, good results are achieved when the remedy corresponds to the characteristics of the person as well as the shape and appearance of the warts. Acid nitricum, Thuja, Anti crud, Causticum, Dulcamera and Ferr picricum are helpful.

Xeroderma Pigmentosum (Sunburn)

Xeroderma pigmentosum, which is commonly known as XP, is an inherited condition characterized by an extreme sensitivity to ultraviolet (UV) rays from sunlight. This condition mostly affects the eyes and areas of skin exposed to the sun. Some affected individuals also have problems involving the nervous system.

People with XP have a greatly increased risk of developing skin cancer. Without sun protection, about half of the children with this condition develop their first skin cancer by age ten. Most people with XP develop multiple skin cancers during their lifetime.

Symptoms

- Severe sunburn when exposed to only small amounts of sunlight. These often occur during a child's first exposure to sunlight
- Development of many freckles at an early age
- Rough-surfaced growths (solar keratoses) and skin cancers
- Eyes that are painfully sensitive to the sun and may easily become irritated, bloodshot and clouded
- Blistering or freckling on minimum sun exposure
- Telangiectasia (spider veins)
- Limited growth of hair on chest and legs
- Scaly skin
- Xeroderma (dry skin)
- Irregular dark spots on the skin
- Corneal ulcerations

Holistic Approach

Ayurveda: Treatments such as Ksheeradhara, Kashayadhara, Lepanam and Navarakizhi along with herbs such as manjista, haridra, kumari and lodhra help to speed up the healing process and soothe the skin.

Naturopathy: Treatments such as herbal packs, steam bath, massage therapy and circular jet.

Yoga: Tadasana, Shashankasana, Balasana and Yoga nidra.

Follow-up: Aloe vera gel application, cold water shower and coconut oil application.

Diet: Aloe vera juice (empty stomach), mixed vegetable juice, soaked nuts, curds (avoid at night) and coconut water.

Homeopathy: Homeopathy offers relief to the patient by reducing the intensity of severe symptoms such as itching, redness and burning, and it reduces the risk of blister formation. Homeopathic medicine also helps in the treatment of chronic complaints arising due to prolonged sun exposure. Homeopathic remedies help to improve your immunity, reduce hypersensitive reactions and promote healing. Some medicines used are Belladonna, Apis, Cantharids, Nat mur, Sepia and Alumina.

Yeast Infection

A vaginal yeast infection is a fungal infection that causes irritation, discharge and intense itchiness of the vagina and the vulva—the tissues at the vaginal opening.

Candidiasis is an infection caused by a yeast (a type of fungus) called *Candida*. Candida normally lives on the skin and inside the body usually in the mouth, throat, gut and vagina, without causing any problems. Candida can cause an infection if conditions change inside the vagina to encourage its growth. Hormones, medicines or changes in the immune system can make infection more likely. The common term for candidiasis in the vagina is a vaginal yeast infection. Other names for this infection are vaginal candidiasis, vulvovaginal candidiasis or candidal vaginitis. Many women experience at least two episodes.

Causes

Most women have a vaginal yeast infection at some point of time in their lives. *Candida albicans* is a common type of fungus. It is often found in small amounts in the vagina, mouth, digestive tract and on the skin. Most of the time, it does not cause infection or symptoms. Candida and many other germs that normally live in the vagina keep each other in balance. Sometimes the number of candida increases. This leads to a yeast infection.

This can happen if:

- ❖ You are taking antibiotics used to treat another infection. Antibiotics change the normal balance between germs in the vagina.
- ❖ You are pregnant.
- ❖ You are obese.
- ❖ You have diabetes.
- ❖ You are taking medicines or have an illness that suppresses your immune system.

Symptoms

Yeast infections with discharge look thick and white, like cottage cheese. Other symptoms of a vulvovaginal yeast infection include:

- ❖ Itching, burning or irritation of the vagina or vulva, which is the tissue surrounding the vagina
- ❖ Pain or soreness in the vagina or the vaginal opening
- ❖ Vaginal burning with intercourse or urination
- ❖ A watery discharge
- ❖ A rash

Holistic Approach

Ayurveda: Treatments such as Choornasweda, Dhanyamlasweda, Virechana, Abhyanga, Prakshalana, Swedana and Lepanam are beneficial along with internal medicines, which include Triphala and Nimba, Haridra, which have antifungal properties.

Naturopathy: Treatments such as herbal oil massage therapy, underwater massage with herbal water, steam bath and herbal pack application.

Yoga: Anuloma viloma, Brahamari pranayama, Shavasana, Pranayama, relaxation and meditation techniques.

Follow-up: Coconut oil and camphor application, and bath with Epsom salts.

Diet: Coconut oil (for cooking), turmeric (with warm water), garlic (3–4 pieces, raw), ginger tea (without milk). Avoid starchy foods and sugar.

Homeopathy: Homeopathic remedies are based on the totality of emotional, physical and mental symptoms of the individual. The intensity of itching sensations, colour and odour of vaginal discharges, and general traits of the body are considered while selecting the remedy. Canthris, Kreosotum, Sepia, Kali mur, Belladonna, Alumina and Borax are some remedies.

Zika Virus Infection

Zika virus infection is spread to people primarily through the bite of an infected mosquito. Zika virus can also be spread from a pregnant mother to her child and through sexual contact with an affected partner. Cases of Zika virus transmission via blood transfusion have also been reported. Zika virus outbreaks are currently occurring in many countries.

The illness associated with Zika virus infection is usually mild, with symptoms lasting for several days to a week. The most common symptoms of Zika are fever, rash, joint pain and conjunctivitis (red eyes). No vaccine currently exists to prevent Zika virus infection.

Zika virus is similar to dengue fever, yellow fever and West Nile virus. Carried by infected *Aedes aegypti* mosquitoes, Zika is largely transmitted through bites but can also occur through intrauterine infection.

Symptoms

- Many people infected with the Zika virus won't have symptoms or will only have mild symptoms.
- Your doctor may order a blood or urine test to help determine if you have Zika.
- There is no specific medicine for Zika.

Holistic Approach

Ayurveda: Internal medications such as Sanjeevani Vati, Sudarshana Ghana Vati and Amrutottara Kashayam along with rest help the body fight against viral infections by improving immunity. Immunity-boosting herbs such as amla, haridra and guduchi are helpful.

Naturopathy: Treatments such as underwater massage, herbal packs, wet sheet pack and sponge bath.

Yoga: Anuloma viloma, Brahmari pranayama, Shavasana, Pranayama, relaxation and meditation techniques.

Follow-up: Hot water bath with neem leaves and coconut oil application.

Diet: Citrus fruits, amla juice (empty stomach), ginger tea (before bed), coconut water (as a snack) and fibre-rich diet.

Homeopathy: Homeopathy is a holistic system of medicine, which is based on individualization and symptom similarity. In epidemic cases, some remedies may be found indicated in most patients called genus epidemicus. Homeopathy can be of great prophylactic help. Eupatorium perfolatum, Rhus tox and Belladonna can be safely used against Zika virus infection.

CHAPTER 2

The A–Z of Wellness

Asafoetida (Hing)

What

Grandma's answer to all stomach ailments, this pungent-smelling sap or dried latex is native to central Asia, Iran and Afghanistan. It is never consumed directly; it is always added to dishes.

Wonders

Age-old remedy for stomach ailments such as gas, bloating and irritable bowel syndrome; helps relieve asthma; lowers BP, relieves menstrual pain; fixes headaches; antidote for insect bites; makes skin radiant and is a natural hair conditioner.

Dr Mathai says

Pregnant and breastfeeding women should avoid this to prevent miscarriage and bleeding disorders in infants.

Aerobics

What

High-intensity rhythmic exercise that works on all areas of the body and is performed usually with a group of people to music.

Wonders

Strengthens heart muscle and lungs; lowers BP and cholesterol; boosts immune system; burns calories and eases stress and anxiety.

Dr Mathai says

Those with a history of heart or respiratory problems and joint disorders or those who recently had surgery should avoid aerobics. Heavy exercises are best avoided before nightfall as the body begins to slow down. Hence, it should be completed before sunset.

Almonds

What

One of the best anti-ageing nuts, almonds are native to central Asia and perhaps the Mediterranean. It is now mainly cultivated in the Middle East, Italy, Spain, Greece and California (the US), which produces over 70 per cent of the world's crop.

Wonders

The magnesium and calcium found in almonds are two vital nutrients for bone health. It is rich in antioxidants and vitamin E; lowers cholesterol; significantly reduces the risk of breast and colon cancer and osteoporosis; keeps the heart healthy; checks blood sugar and BP; nourishes the skin and is good for memory.

Dr Mathai says

Almonds can be consumed in any form—powdered and added to your oats and cereals or atta flour (to make rotis), in dishes, coloured rice, or simply chew whole almonds. Yet another way to consume almonds is to soak them overnight and consume them first thing in the morning before your morning cuppa.

AMLA (INDIAN GOOSEBERRY)

What

Amla, which is rich in Vitamin C, is extremely sour and nutritious, this light-green fruit is often used in Ayurvedic medicines.

Wonders

A super fruit for building immunity and protecting the body against infections, it enriches hair growth and nourishes skin; aids digestion and improves appetite; flushes out unwanted toxins by increasing urination; controls diabetes; is anti-ageing; strengthens heart muscles; boosts blood circulation and improves eyesight.

Dr Mathai says

Amla can be consumed in many forms—juice, pickle (not too spicy), or simply chew whole amla. If you have a sore throat or are prone to getting one, soak amla in warm water and have it.

Bananas

What

An extremely popular fruit crop, banana is widely grown and consumed across the world. Available throughout the year, the highly nutritional fruit is full of carbs and calories. It is believed to have been first domesticated in South-east Asia and its consumption is mentioned in early Greek, Latin and Arab writings. Alexander the Great saw bananas on an expedition to India.

Wonders

Loaded with fibre, it gives you the feeling of a full stomach for a longer time; lowers the risk of cardiovascular diseases; checks BP; aids digestion; boosts metabolism; gives relief from piles and fights anaemia.

Dr Mathai says

Eat in moderation, otherwise it can lead to weight gain.

Beetroots

What

The rich purple-coloured root vegetable has a distinct earthy flavour and is of exceptional nutritional value. Classic beetroot recipes include soup and curries. First cultivated by the Romans, it was of high commercial value by the nineteenth century because it could be converted into sugar.

Wonders

Detoxifies the body; is low in calories and almost fat-free; improves blood flow and checks BP. As a potent antioxidant, it prevents heart diseases; boosts immunity; aids digestive function and also fights flakes in hair and itchy scalp.

Dr Mathai says

It is commonly misunderstood that diabetic patients should avoid beetroot as it is sweet, while it actually lowers the risk of diabetic complications.

BADMINTON

What

The extremely popular shuttle game is named after the country estate of the dukes of Beaufort in Gloucestershire, England, where it was first played around 1873. The roots of the sport can be traced back to ancient Greece, China and India. Badminton is derived directly from Poona, which was played by British army officers stationed in India in the 1860s.

Wonders

Playing badminton regularly helps to reduce weight easily; tones muscle and maintains physique; improves metabolism; makes you more alert, agile and productive; strengthens heart muscles; increases bone density; lowers the risk of diabetes and boosts the functioning of the lungs.

Dr Mathai says

A good warm-up before the game always helps.

Broccoli

What

A delicious nutrient-rich vegetable belonging to the cabbage family. Native to the Eastern Mediterranean and Asia Minor, sprouting broccoli was cultivated in Italy in ancient Roman times and was introduced to England and America in the 1700s. The dark-green vegetable can be eaten both fresh and cooked.

Wonders

Has anti-cancer and immunity-boosting contents; draws cholesterol out of the body; checks allergy and inflammation; is a rich antioxidant; contains high calcium and vitamin K levels that boost bone health; protects blood vessels and checks BP; aids digestion and prevents constipation; protects the skin and eyes and has anti-ageing properties.

Dr Mathai says

Watch out for allergies.

Bathing

What

A good shower is all you need to start a good day! Bathing has been an integral part of human health and there are different ways people across the world love to do it. Scandinavians take plunges in cool water after time in a sauna, while the Romans' love for baths actually gave birth to huge bathing complexes with under-floor heating and a range of temperatures, some of which are still standing today.

Wonders

Lifts mood; helps soothe your skin, boosts oxygen uptake; relieves chest congestion and cold, and a bath before bed induces better sleep. A warm bath relieves pain and swelling and increases lung capacity.

Dr Mathai says

Don't bathe with extremely hot water at night. You could end up feeling more alert and on edge, which isn't conducive to a peaceful night's rest.

Carrots (gajar)

What

The root vegetable widely used across the world was first cultivated thousands of years ago in Afghanistan as a small, forked purple or yellow root, much different from the one we know today. The orange carrot popular today was developed by Dutch farmers in the sixteenth and seventeenth centuries.

Wonders

Contains beta-carotene, which is believed to reduce the risk of a range of cancers; improves eye health; regulates blood cholesterol; checks diabetes and BP; boosts immunity; aids in digestion and significantly cuts the risk of stroke.

Dr Mathai says

Overeating carrots should be avoided as they are rich in Vitamin A. Those taking medications derived from Vitamin A for acne or psoriasis must avoid eating carrots in large amounts.

Cherries

What

Cherries are small, round, deep-red stone fruit that has its origins in the region between the Black and Caspian Seas. Turkey is the world's leading producer of cherries. Sweet cherries are usually eaten as they come, while tart cherries are used more in cooking. All cherries have a stone in the middle which must be removed before eating or cooking.

Wonders

Improves sleep; facilitates weight loss; checks BP; cuts the risk of heart ailments; reduces inflammation; makes skin and hair healthy; prevents acidity and indigestion by maintaining pH balance and is a superb energy-boosting fruit.

Dr Mathai says

An amazing fruit; just check for allergies if you are sensitive.

Cycling

What

The two-wheeled bicycle was invented in Germany in 1817 by Baron Karl von Drais as a walking vehicle, which he moved ahead by pushing his feet against the ground. The crude device eventually transformed into a modern-day transport wonder with immense health benefits.

Wonders

Helps incorporate physical activity into daily life; tones muscle; improves cardiovascular function; prevents and reduces arthritis; burns calories and boosts body stamina and endurance capacity. Pedalling is good for better functioning of the heart, brain and blood vessels.

Dr Mathai says

Consult a doctor before you take on cycling if you have a heart condition, arthritis or thinning bones. And always wear a helmet!

CUMIN (JEERA)

What

One of the oldest and most widely used spices in cooking in India and other Asian countries, Africa and South America. Cumin seeds were excavated at a site in Syria back in 2000 BC. Even the Bible has a mention of cumin seeds.

Wonders

Improves digestion; helps bolster the body's immune system; treats anaemia; is an excellent detoxifying agent; keeps the skin firm and moist and has anti-congestive properties. It is antiviral and antibacterial and improves the symptoms of piles and irritable bowel syndrome.

Dr Mathai says

May lower blood sugar levels in some and slow down the clotting of blood.

Celery

What

A crunchy stalk of vegetable, which is most commonly found in soups, salads or as a garnish in certain dishes. This globally cultivated plant traces its origins to the Mediterranean and North Africa.

Wonders

Lowers cholesterol levels and reduces BP; fights cancer; prevents urinary tract infection in women; manages diabetic symptoms; helps reduce inflammation and joint pain; relieves migraine and asthma, and boosts eye health.

Dr Mathai says

Just check for allergies. It may cause severe allergic reactions in some people.

Eggs

What

Eggs have been a part of the human diet for thousands of years. It is not only a wholesome food source in itself but is also a key ingredient in a range of delicacies across the world. A single egg has enough nutrients to develop a single cell into a baby chick!

Wonders

Has high protein content and essential vitamins that help in the proper growth of the body, and essential minerals such as iron, zinc and phosphorus, which are required for a healthy body. It increases good cholesterol; lowers the risk of heart diseases; boosts cognitive ability; strengthens the bones and muscles, and reduces the risk of eye conditions such as cataract.

Dr Mathai says

Eat in moderation, just an egg a day works well.

Figs

What

Loaded with calcium, figs grow in dry and rocky locations and date back to the Neolithic age (9400–9200 BC). Said to be a common food source for the Romans, figs lessen the risk of osteoporosis as they help to maintain the calcium level in bones.

Wonders

A solid toner for intestines, figs are rich in minerals, including potassium, calcium, magnesium and iron. Often recommended by doctors to increase the vitamin A and K content in the body, they act as a natural laxative due to the high fibre content.

Dr Mathai says

Eating excessive amounts of figs is likely to have a laxative effect and so they should be enjoyed in moderation only. Figs counter the urinary excretion for those consuming saltier food.

Fenugreek

What

This wonder herb is used in soaps, cooking and in shampoos for good hair growth. The all-encompassing seed's origin dates back thousands of years.

Wonders

With the incidence of diabetes increasing, the consumption of fenugreek regularly helps in improving insulin function. In addition to helping lower cholesterol levels, this herb helps with heartburn and inflammation reduction. It also acts as a cooling agent for the hair.

Dr Mathai says

Excess consumption can lead to diarrhoea across age groups. The best way to consume fenugreek leaves is methi rotis or add the seeds to dishes after mashing them.

Fava beans

What

From China to Ecuador to Croatia, the fava bean is a global bean and is consumed with cheese, as a snack or added to dishes in some countries. The origin of this widely consumed bean dates back to 6000 BC, when it became a part of the Eastern Mediterranean diet. They are popular in various parts of the globe and are known by different names in each of these countries.

Wonders

The bean is as good for an eighty-year-old as much as it is for a newborn. Rich in Levodopa (L-dopa) which treats Parkinson's, the bean may help with symptoms of Parkinson's disease. Rich in plant protein and antioxidants, vitamins and minerals, regular consumption of fava beans can aid digestion and lower cholesterol levels. The folate content in the beans helps promote healthy foetal development.

Dr Mathai says

Very frequent consumption of fava beans can cause stomach bloating, flatulence and diarrhoea. It is more important to eat cooked beans than raw ones.

French beans

What

These ubiquitous green beans date back to 1894 and are a super vegetable for hair, skin and bones. The bean's ancestors originated in South and Central America. It was a Spanish conquest that brought the beans to Europe and eventually to other parts of the world.

Wonders

With nearly 100 varieties, they are an excellent source of vitamin K and are loaded with protein, omega-3 fatty acids, iron, vitamin B6 and vitamin E. Low in calories and containing no saturated fat, they are a fantastic source of vitamin C, folic acid and fibre.

Dr Mathai says

The bean is a boon for women as it gives flawless skin and aids in weight loss. Regular consumption maintains the red blood cell count, keeps the arteries clear of clogs and prevents the growth of cancer cells.

Fish

What

The modern English word for fish comes from the word *fisc* and historically is an answer to daily protein for the human body. Regular consumption of fish has proved to fight micronutrient deficiencies.

Wonders

High in omega-3 fatty acids and low in fat, it helps maintain a healthy heart by regulating blood clotting and vessel constriction to reduce cardiac arrhythmia. The protein content in the fish reduces tissue inflammation, thereby reducing symptoms of rheumatoid arthritis.

Dr Mathai says

Those with seafood allergies must be cautious about the regular consumption of fish. Though fish is low in fat, eating fish that breeds in contaminated water may increase cancer risk. Consume only high-quality fish.

GUAVA (AMROOD)

What

The humble sweet fruit is a powerhouse of nutrients. Mostly eaten raw or in the form of jams, juice and jellies, the fruit is believed to have originated in Mexico or Central America.

Wonders

One of the richest sources of vitamin C, it prevents cold and viral infections; lowers the risk of prostate and breast cancer; controls diarrhoea and treats constipation; helps lose weight; keeps hormone levels in check; boosts brain function; improves eyesight and checks BP and diabetes.

Dr Mathai says

Medicines with a large concentration of guava may not be suitable for pregnant or breastfeeding women as it is mostly eaten raw, which can cause infection or diarrhoea.

Ginger (adrak)

What

An ancient spice and popular cooking ingredient in cuisines in India and other parts of Asia. Its root or underground stem can be used raw, dried, powdered, as oil or juice. Native to the Indo–Malaysian rainforests, it's commonly cultivated in India, Jamaica, Fiji, Indonesia and Australia.

Wonders

Aids digestion; a natural remedy for cold and flu; prevents nausea; lowers the risk of certain cancers; provides relief from menstrual cramps; regulates sugar levels and lowers diabetes risk.

Dr Mathai says

A high intake may worsen symptoms of acid reflux, irritate the mouth and cause diarrhoea.

GRATITUDE

What

A thankful appreciation of what we receive, tangible or intangible. Expressing thanks may be one of the simplest ways to feel better.

Wonders

Gratitude is strongly associated with more happiness. It helps people feel more positive emotions, relish good experiences, deal with adversity in life, improve health and build strong relationships.

Dr Mathai says

Gratitude helps us focus on what we have instead of what we lack.

Ghee (clarified butter)

What

Ghee has been used in cuisines in India and the Middle East and in Ayurvedic medicines since ancient times. It's a pure combination of fats without any milk residue.

Wonders

Strengthens immune system; boosts energy levels; is good for lactose-intolerant people; keeps the heart healthy; reduces inflammation, particularly in the gastrointestinal tract and aids eye health.

Dr Mathai says

It's pure fat, so use it moderately!

Garlic (lahsun)

What

A pungent-smelling herb that has been used across the world as a food-flavouring agent and in traditional medicines since ancient times. Records indicate its use when the Giza pyramids were built about 5000 years ago.

Wonders

Alleviates cold and cough; lowers cholesterol levels; relieves earaches; aids digestion; purifies blood and detoxifies the body; has antibacterial, antiparasitic and anticarcinogenic properties; cures splinter cuts; cures eye infection and prevents hair loss.

Dr Mathai says

Excess intake may cause irritation in the digestive system and definitely bad breath!

Herbs

What

From soups to perfumes to sauces, they are used everywhere. The word 'herb' comes from the Latin word *herba*, meaning grass, green stalks or blades. They are used as food, medicine and even for spiritual reasons in many countries.

Wonders

Virtually every herb has a health benefit. Garlic, fenugreek and lemongrass help lower cholesterol, while basil, oregano, mint, flaxseed and cinnamon can help control blood sugar or insulin activity. Fresh herbs contain higher antioxidant levels compared to processed or dried herbs. They can also help reduce blood clots and have anti-inflammatory and anti-tumour properties.

Dr Mathai says

One needs to be cautious about herb formulations as they may lead to side effects on the liver and heart. Consult your physician if herbs are being used for treating some ailment.

Honey

What

Honey's use and production have a long and varied history as an ancient activity. Several cave paintings of honey-hunting date back at least 8000 years. It remained a medicine for centuries in many countries. Over 4000 years ago, honey was used in traditional Ayurvedic medicine where it was thought to be effective in treating indigestion and imbalances in the body.

Wonders

From treating cough in children to being used as an antibiotic to treating wounds and burns, the nectar is a must-have in every kitchen across the globe. The spiritual and therapeutic use of honey (for indigestion and imbalances in the body) is documented in both the Vedas and Ayurvedic texts some 4000 years ago. Honey can reduce the upward flow of stomach acid and undigested food that causes acid reflux and heartburn, and has been used to treat a wide array of illnesses, ailments and injuries.

Dr Mathai says

Be wary of buying honey everywhere. Pure honey (raw honey), if not of good quality, can lead to diarrhoea and vomiting.

Honeydew melon

What

Honeydew melon, or honey melon, is a fruit that belongs to the melon species Cucumis melo (muskmelon). Honeydew melon is available worldwide and can be eaten by itself or used in desserts, salads, snacks and soups. Though its greatest appeal may be its flavour, honeydew is also nutritious and has several benefits.

Wonders

From magnesium to fibre to proteins to vitamins, this melon has it all in a cup. With its low-sodium levels and being a potassium-rich fruit, it helps maintain healthy BP levels. Loaded with vitamin K, folate and magnesium, it is good for strong bones.

Dr Mathai says

Regular consumption of this fruit can even lower the risk of diabetes.

Hazelnut

What

This nut, which dates back to 6000 BC, is a favourite among children and adults. There is evidence that about 8000 years ago, these nuts were processed in Mesolithic sites.

Wonders

As a good source of dietary fibre, this nut encourages regular bowel movements and helps prevent constipation. Being rich in antioxidants, regular consumption of hazelnut reduces cell damage and therefore eases inflammation.

Dr Mathai says

The best way to eat hazelnut is unroasted to retain all its nutrients. The nut has anti-cancer properties too but be warned about allergies.

HATHA YOGA

What

Some haṭha yoga techniques can be traced back to the first century CE, in texts such as the Sanskrit epics. The earliest mention of haṭha yoga is in Buddhist texts, mainly Tantric works from the eighth century onwards.

Wonders

Bringing flexibility to virtually every part of your body, hatha yoga awakens all the chakras in the body. Doing hatha yoga regularly builds your core strength and lubricates your bones (due to the regular asanas). The Surya Namaskar in hatha yoga treats your backache and relieves stress for today's overworked generation.

Dr Mathai says

Half an hour of hatha yoga every day is a pathway to health. And since it combines power yoga, this yoga aids weight loss too.

Jatropha

What

Jatropha curcas, also known as the 'physic nut', is a perennial shrub that is native to Central America but grows widely in Africa and Asia. The seed oil of this poisonous plant is used to produce high-grade bio-diesel fuel.

Wonders

Used to treat various ailments, mostly external, such as joint and muscle aches (arthritis and rheumatism) as it has anti-inflammatory properties. It also treats snakebites and is used as an insecticide.

Dr Mathai says

Must be used with great caution and only on a doctor's advice.

JUNIPER BERRIES

What

Juniper berries are small blue or purple berries from the juniper evergreen plant. They are also known as gin berries due to the fact that they are used for flavour in gin, bitters and liqueurs.

Wonders

With antioxidant properties, it decreases inflammation of a gout attack; reduces joint, arthritic and rheumatic pains and aids in the functioning of the digestive system. It also helps get rid of the excess water and waste from the kidneys and bladder. A superb body detoxifier, it is also used in making herbal tea.

Dr Mathai says

Prolonged use can cause kidney irritation. Also, avoid juniper berries if you are pregnant or breastfeeding because they can cause miscarriages.

Jogging

What

An activity of running at a steady, gentle pace as a form of physical exercise that boosts well-being, both physically and mentally.

Wonders

Helps burn calories and develop muscles; good for the respiratory system as it increases lung capacity; reduces stress levels and the risk of cancer, and boosts memory.

Dr Mathai says

Avoid eating right before jogging, drink plenty of water and wear comfortable clothes while jogging.

Jal Neti

What

A nasal cleansing yogic process where salted lukewarm water is used to remove the congestion and blockages of nasal as well as respiratory regions.

Wonders

Helps in curing sinusitis; prevents cold, cough and allergic sneezing; alleviates chronic headaches and migraine; cures insomnia; sharpens memory and treats eye-related ailments.

Dr Mathai says

Should be initially practised under the guidance of a yoga expert. Remember to breathe through the mouth throughout the practice.

Jackfruit

What

An exotic tropical fruit with a subtle, sweet flavour that is consumed in many parts of the world. It can be eaten in a variety of ways.

Wonders

Contains a variety of antioxidants that help prevent chronic diseases such as diabetes and heart conditions, improve skin health and slow ageing. Boosts immunity and reduces the risk of viral infections.

Dr Mathai says

No major risk is associated, with the exception of those who are allergic to it.

Lemon (nimbu)

What

Believed to have originated in Assam (India) and parts of Myanmar and China, the yellow-green fruit is an excellent source of vitamin C. While lemonade is a popular beverage across the world, lemon is commonly added to salads, curries and chutneys. The early explorers took lemons first on long voyages to help prevent or treat scurvy.

Wonders

Checks high BP; helps reduce weight; relieves fever and cold; prevents kidney stone formation; boosts immunity; helps fade skin scars; stops nose bleeds; checks dandruff and gives shine to hair; soothes toothache and cleanses the teeth; and eases the pain of sunburn and bee stings.

Dr Mathai says

A superb commonly available fruit. Just avoid over-intake as it is high in acid.

Lotus Pose (Padmasana)

What

In this popular meditation and yogic posture, the legs are crossed and the feet are placed on opposite thighs with the spine vertical and lengthened. The formation of the legs in this posture resembles that of lotus petals.

Wonders

Opens and releases the hips; improves spine health and posture; reduces the risk of backache; eases menstruation symptoms; calms the mind; stretches the ankles and knees; optimizes the functioning of the body; and purifies and harmonizes physical, mental and spiritual well-being.

Dr Mathai says

Avoid if you have a knee or ankle injury.

Lentils (dal)

What

High-protein and high-fibre-rich edible pulses or seeds are one of the oldest known sources of food, dating back to over 9000 years. Various kinds of lentils are consumed much more in Asia, particularly in India, daily.

Wonders

Checks diabetes and BP; reduces cancer risk; superb source of vitamins and minerals; aids digestion and metabolism; helps in optimal brain functioning and aids in weight management. Sprouted lentils aid in muscle-building and prevent cell and gene damage.

Dr Mathai says

High intake may affect the functioning of the kidneys and can also lead to gas formation and constipation.

LAUGHTER

What

'Laughter is the best medicine.' This is something we all have heard, and there are reasons behind it not many are aware of. A good laugh indeed has far-ranging benefits.

Wonders

A simple natural way to work out various body muscles, it lowers stress hormones; checks high BP; boosts memory and lifts mood; helps ease pain; reduces anxiety and negative emotions; and stimulates blood flow and oxygenation in the body.

Dr Mathai says

So, laugh out loud!

Lychee

What

Soft whitish-pink pulpy fruit with a distinct aroma that has been cultivated for over 4000 years in China. It grows in tropical and subtropical regions and is mainly produced in South-east Asia, China, India and southern Africa.

Wonders

Strengthens the body's immune system; aids digestion; prevents the spread of viruses such as herpes; promotes blood circulation; regulates BP and the body's fluid balance; protects skin against UV rays; aids weight loss and reduces the risk of cancer.

Dr Mathai says

Eating excessive unripe lychees on an empty stomach can cause symptoms of fever and vomiting.

Mindfulness

What

The basic human ability to be fully present, aware of where we are and what we're doing, and not overly reactive or overwhelmed by what's going on around us.

Wonders

Reduces anxiety; improves cognitive abilities; helps the brain reduce distractions; induces better sleep; helps relieve stress and BP; and improves general well-being.

Dr Mathai says

Mindfulness is a quality that every human being already possesses. You just have to learn how to access it.

Mango

What

Succulent and refreshing, mango finds mentions as 'amra' in the Brihadaranyaka Upanishad, believed to be written between 1000 and 700 BC. Considered indigenous to Eastern Asia, Myanmar and Assam in India, the name mango is most likely derived from the Malayalam 'manna', which the Portuguese adopted as 'manga' when they came to Kerala in 1498 for the spice trade. The tree was not introduced to the West until about 1700.

Wonders

Helps in digestion and promotes a healthy gut; boosts immunity as a powerful antioxidant; beneficial for anaemic people; beta-carotene in it promotes eye health; regulates cholesterol levels; good for healthy skin; has anti-diabetic properties though it's sweet, and helps in gaining weight.

Dr Mathai says

Eating mango as a whole and in its natural form is the best way to enjoy it.

Mushroom

What

Not much was known about this delicious little fungi before the French introduced mushrooms into their haute cuisine. Today, it can be seen in dishes ranging from salads to vegetables served across the world. Button mushroom is the most commonly consumed variety.

Wonders

Lowers cholesterol levels; gives energy as they are rich in vitamin B; strengthens the bones; is ideal for diabetic patients; boosts the immune system and memory; reduces the risk of neurological illness due to the antioxidants in it and helps you feel young.

Dr Mathai says

Every mushroom must be accurately identified. Consumption of poisonous wild mushrooms can be fatal.

MUSTARD

What

The pungent spicy condiment made from seeds of the mustard plant is used across the world in dishes and sandwiches. The use of mustard seeds as a spice is described in Indian and Sumerian texts dating back to 3000 BC. Hippocrates and other ancient physicians used mustard for medicinal purposes. The principal types are yellow and brown.

Wonders

Excellent decongestant and expectorant as it clears mucus in the air passage, mustard oil relieves body pain; balances cholesterol levels; prevents bad breath; fights various kinds of cancers; aids metabolism; promotes healthy hair and skin; and has an anti-fungal effect against ringworm.

Dr Mathai says

Mustard seeds can be allergic. Use cooking oil moderately as it contains high levels of erucic acid.

Mountaineering

What

Can seem intimidating for the uninitiated but it brings along tremendous mental and physical benefits, and at a very low cost. It is no wonder that people all over the world do it.

Wonders

Boosts the heart function and lung capacity; helps maintain BP; increases blood oxygen levels; improves coordination between eyes, hands and feet; tones muscles; increases confidence and helps conquer fear.

Dr Mathai says

Do remember to undergo basic training before you start climbing.

Neem

What

A popular medicinal herb that's been part of traditional remedies dating back almost 5000 years. It has more than 130 biologically active compounds and is proven to have antiviral and antibacterial properties, along with being a powerful immunostimulant.

Wonders

Heals wounds and insect bites; boosts immunity; is anti-carcinogenic; neem water fights dandruff in hair; helps reduce eye irritation, tiredness and redness, dark spots and chronic ulcers; treats skin disorders such as itching and eczema; purifies blood; treats intestinal worms and keeps gums and teeth healthy.

Dr Mathai says

Neem is generally safe for use but check for related allergies or sensitivity, particularly in children and pregnant women.

NETBALL

What

Similar to basketball, although the rules, equipment and team numbers differ. The sport is particularly popular in Commonwealth nations.

Wonders

Improves hand-eye coordination; builds muscle strength; burns calories; boosts the cardiovascular system; increases alertness, thereby enhancing decision-making skills.

Dr Mathai says

Wear appropriate clothing and avoid playing on wet courts to keep injuries at bay.

NUTMEG

What

Nutmeg is a popular spice made from the seed of the nutmeg tree or Myristica fragrans, native to the Spice Islands of Indonesia.

Wonders

Relieves joint and muscle pain; induces sleep and treats insomnia; aids digestion; stimulates nerves in the brain as an aphrodisiac; prevents bad breath and toothaches; great for the skin and regulates blood circulation and BP.

Dr Mathai says

Breastfeeding and pregnant women should avoid intake of nutmeg in large doses.

Olive

What

An integral part of the Mediterranean diet, olives belong to a special group of fruits called drupes. Various kinds of olives and their oils are used in salads, pasta and other delicacies. They have been cultivated in parts of the Mediterranean—including Crete and Syria—for at least 5000 years.

Wonders

Reduces risk of cardiovascular diseases; helps prevent breast and colon cancer and gallstones; aids in weight loss; protects skin from UV rays and premature ageing; boosts metabolism and digestion; is a rich source of iron; has anti-inflammatory properties and stops eye degeneration.

Dr Mathai says

Just check for allergies, otherwise they are safe.

Onion

What

This humble vegetable holds centre stage in meals across the world and has been a part of the human diet for thousands of years. In Egypt, they were worshipped and used in burial rituals. Cultivated globally, China is its largest producer.

Wonders

Strengthens the immune system; lowers bad cholesterol and keeps the heart healthy; reduces the risk of cancer, particularly stomach and colorectal; manages blood sugar; is effective against cold and heat stroke; has antibacterial and anti-inflammatory properties; improves skin and hair; and slows down nose bleeds.

Dr Mathai says

Watch out for bad breath and teary eyes!

Om

What

Pronounced 'Aum', Om is a universal sound chanted by yogis and spiritual masters for ages. Considered the most sacred sound, it embodies the essence of the entire universe.

Wonders

When chanted, it creates strong, blissful energy vibrations, calming the body and mind. It allays depression; boosts concentration and mental alertness; balances emotions; checks negativity and improves lung function. Regular and proper chanting improves the spinal cord function, soothes stomach ache and controls BP.

Dr Mathai says

'Om' connects us to everything around us. Chant it to see the transformation!

Orange

What

One of the most widely cultivated fruit trees in the world, it originated thousands of years ago in the region from southern China to Indonesia, and from there it came to India. The US, China and Brazil are among the largest orange-producing nations.

Wonders

Reduces the risk of cancer; prevents cold and recurrent ear infection; protects the skin and checks ageing; keeps BP under check; lowers cholesterol levels; controls blood sugar; aids digestion; improves vision; prevents irritable bowel syndrome and treats constipation.

Dr Mathai says

Eat in moderation as it is rich in potassium and can affect those with kidney conditions.

Papaya

What

Papayas grow in tropical climates and are native to Mexico, but India produces the most papayas globally. (Source: Food and Agriculture Organization of the United Nations)

Wonders

Promotes eye health and wards off macular degeneration; beta-carotene in it prevents asthma; reduces cancer risk; strengthens bones; lowers blood sugar levels; aids digestion and prevents constipation; reduces the risk of cardiovascular diseases; reduces chronic inflammation and helps heal wounds. Papaya is also great for hair and skin.

Dr Mathai says

Unripe and semi-ripe papaya should be avoided during pregnancy because it can cause uterine contractions. Extracts from papaya seeds can lower male fertility.

Parsley

What

Widely used as a fresh culinary herb or dried spice in American, European and Middle-Eastern cooking.

Wonders

Prevents breast cancer; soothes inflammation due to the antioxidants in it; prevents wrinkles and enhances skin health; strengthens bones; aids digestion and reduces bloating. Helps treat urinary tract infections and kidney stones, and fights heart and eye conditions.

Dr Mathai says

Avoid the consumption of parsley during pregnancy and breastfeeding. Those suffering from bleeding disorders, too, should avoid its intake as it slows down the process of blood clotting.

Pilates

What

A popular form of exercise that concentrates on posture, balance and flexibility, improving general fitness and overall well-being.

Wonders

Helps gain and maintain good body posture; especially beneficial for those suffering from lower back pain; tones muscles and flattens stomach; improves physical balance and relieves stress.

Dr Mathai says

May not be right for people with unstable BP, herniated discs, severe osteoporosis and a risk of blood clots.

Potato

What

These edible tubers are among the world's most savoured and widely used vegetables. Many don't know that potatoes are naturally gluten-free and have zero cholesterol.

Wonders

Relieves inflammation associated with arthritis; reduces stomach acidity, and helps regulate BP and calm the nerves. The fibre, potassium and antioxidants in it are great for heart health. It also aids digestion; promotes sleep; strengthens bones; helps treat acne, dark circles and puffy eyes; boosts cognitive functions and relieves premenstrual symptoms.

Dr Mathai says

If prepared well (read baked, mashed or tossed in salads), they can work wonders. It's the way we cook and consume potatoes that isn't really right always.

Pranayama

What

The popular yogic practice of controlling the breath, the source of our vital life force.

Wonders

Boosts blood circulation; keeps heart ailments away; relaxes the body and mind; improves concentration; relieves stress and hypertension; cures asthma, headache and migraine; improves blood circulation as well as the functioning of reproductive organs.

Dr Mathai says

Morning is the best time to do pranayama and on an empty stomach for better results.

Strawberries

What

A member of the rose family, strawberry plants are runners and are not produced by seeds. They are also not actually fruits as their seeds are on the outside. Native to many parts of the world, strawberries have been relished since Roman times.

Wonders

Prevents heart diseases and cuts cholesterol; reduces the risk of arthritis and cancer; helps regulate the functioning of the nervous system; checks high BP; boosts the immune system; lowers the risk of eye ailments; aids digestion and prevents constipation.

Dr Mathai says

If you are allergic to birch pollen, you are most likely to develop a secondary food allergy to strawberries.

Sweet Potato

What

Native to Central and South America, this starchy, sweet root vegetable has been consumed since prehistoric times with relics dating back 10,000 years found in Peruvian caves. Christopher Columbus brought them to Europe. China is the world's leading producer of sweet potatoes.

Wonders

Aids digestion and checks constipation; reduces the risk of cancer; boosts the immune system; has anti-inflammatory properties; aids in curing stomach ulcers; improves eye health; maintains the body's water balance and regulates blood sugar.

Dr Mathai says

Boiling sweet potatoes with the skin intact is more beneficial than baking or frying.

Sleep

What

A good night's sleep is vital to our physical and emotional well-being. We all know how going without sleep for too long makes us feel terrible.

Wonders

Reduces stress levels; boosts memory; lowers BP; strengthens the immune system; helps maintain weight; lifts mood; lowers diabetes risk; acts as a painkiller, and keeps you mentally and physically agile.

Dr Mathai says

A good seven-hour sleep is not just a good idea, it's essential.

Surya Namaskar

What

The ancient yogic technique of showing gratitude to the sun, the source of all life on Earth. It is a set of twelve different postures that brings the body, breath and mind together.

Wonders

Strengthens the back; keeps the skin glowing and supple; aids digestion and keeps the gut healthy; helps lose weight; strengthens muscles and joints; regulates the menstrual cycle; checks hormonal imbalance; clears blocked pathways in the body, aids sound sleep; checks anxiety and BP; protects against heart ailments and aids positivity.

Dr Mathai says

The ideal time to practise is the morning when the sun is visible, and on an empty stomach.

Spinach

What

One of the most popular leafy vegetables, it is a rich source of minerals, vitamins, pigments and phytonutrients. Spinach can be eaten raw as a part of salads, cooked or sautéed, as a side dish vegetable or added to soups and stews. It is native to the Middle East and was cultivated in Persia thousands of years ago from where it was brought to China and later Europe.

Wonders

Rich in vitamin K, it strengthens the bones by stabilizing the calcium content; beta-carotene in it boosts eyesight and the body's immunity; helps in blood clotting; lowers BP; checks heart attacks and strokes; helps in healthy foetal growth and keeps you energized by maintaining the magnesium levels in the body.

Dr Mathai says

Avoid eating spinach if you are undergoing dialysis, are diabetic or are on anticoagulants.

Tamarind (imli)

What

A delicious sweet and sour fruit that has a wide variety of medicinal and culinary uses. The tamarind tree is native to tropical regions in Africa, specifically Sudan.

Wonders

Aids digestion; boosts the immune system; helps manage diabetes; improves nerve function; promotes blood circulation; checks BP and cholesterol; and relieves joint pain, inflammation and gout.

Dr Mathai says

Tamarind lowers BP and is a blood thinner.

Turmeric

What

The yellow-coloured ancient spice is used mainly in cooking and has a host of medicinal benefits.

Wonders

Helps manage pain and inflammation particularly related to rheumatoid and osteo arthritis; lowers blood sugar and cholesterol levels; is anti-cancer and checks tumour development; controls symptoms of irritable bowel syndrome, anxiety and depression; and boosts the memory of Alzheimer's patients. Its antibacterial properties also help control skin problems such as acne.

Dr Mathai says

Avoid turmeric during summer as it can cause dysentery and diarrhoea owing to its hot potency.

Tai Chi

What

A non-competitive martial art known for its self-defence techniques and health benefits. As a form of exercise, it combines gentle physical exercise and stretching with mindfulness.

Wonders

Improves balance; helps prevents trips and falls in the elderly; and manages pain and cognitive function in people with or without chronic conditions. Other possible benefits include improved sleep quality and an enhanced immune system, and it boosts cardiovascular health, mental health and cognitive functions.

Dr Mathai says

Although a low-impact activity, people should seek medical advice before starting, particularly the elderly, pregnant or those experiencing back pain and osteoporosis.

Tomato

What

Among the most popular and consumed fresh-market vegetables across the world, it is an intensely nutritious plant food.

Wonders

Rich in vitamin C and antioxidants, it helps prevent cancer, particularly prostate and colon cancer. It helps maintain BP and boosts heart health; checks the formation of kidney stones; lowers blood sugar levels; reduces constipation; protects the eyes and boosts skin health. The abundant folic acid in tomatoes is beneficial for pregnant women and infants.

Dr Mathai says

Remember to wash tomatoes before eating as they are known to have high levels of pesticide residue, or go organic.

Thyme

What

Thyme is a Mediterranean herb with dietary, medicinal and ornamental uses.

Wonders

Improves bronchitis symptoms and reduces coughing. It is consumed orally for colic, arthritis, stomach pain, dyspraxia (a movement disorder in kids) and skin disorders. It is also used to increase urine flow. Thyme oil is used as a germ-killer in mouthwashes and liniments.

Dr Mathai says

In some people, it can upset the digestive system and cause headaches or dizziness, and can slow down blood clotting. Those allergic to oregano may also be allergic to thyme.

Vanilla

What

The first choice of ice-cream eaters across the globe, vanilla is a member of the orchid family and the second-most expensive spice in the world (after saffron). A native of South and Central America and the Caribbean, the first people to have cultivated vanilla seem to have been the Totonacs of Mexico's east coast. By the eighteenth century, the French were using vanilla to flavour ice cream—a treat discovered by Thomas Jefferson in the 1780s, when he lived in Paris as the American minister to France.

Wonders

Reduces cholesterol levels and the risk of heart attacks and strokes; antioxidants in it stimulate the body's natural regrowth; boosts the immune system; soothes inflammation in the body; fights acne and helps in weight loss. Drinking vanilla herbal tea aids digestion; its extract mixed with warm water helps with cold and cough. Vanilla essential oil treats split hair ends and hair loss.

Dr Mathai says

Most vanilla you consume today is synthetic and not naturally grown.

VINEGAR

What

Natural vinegar is made of fruits such as apple, grape or Indian blueberry. Used in cooking, baking, salad dressings and as a preservative, compounds containing vinegar have been used for thousands of years for their healing properties. Known as 'poor man's wine', its use has been found in Egyptian and Babylonian civilizations.

Wonders

Has been used from ancient times to improve strength, detoxify the body, as an antibiotic and for the treatment of scurvy and dandruff. It is presumed to aid weight loss according to some research and prevent an increase in blood sugar levels.

Dr Mathai says

Vinegar should be diluted before use as it is highly acidic.

Watermelon

What

The sweet, cool and refreshing watermelon is native to tropical Africa. It grows on vine-like flowering plants and is rich in vitamins A and C. The fruit was depicted in early Egyptian art as early as 4000 years ago.

Wonders

Helps flush out toxic deposits in the kidney; prevents dehydration and reduces body temperature; regulates BP; lycopene in it reduces the risk of cancer; controls diabetes; improves heart function and prevents age-related eye problems.

Dr Mathai says

Don't eat pre-cut watermelons, particularly on the roadside. It can result in foodborne illness.

Walking

What

Walking is a boon to overall well-being and comes with a host of surprising benefits. Even a few steps every day can take you a long way.

Wonders

Counteracts effects of weight-promoting genes; curbs cravings for sweets; eases arthritis-related pain; reduces the risk of breast cancer; boosts immune function; checks heart diseases; boosts memory and prevents age-related physical problems.

Dr Mathai says

Make it a point to get up every hour or so and walk around your workplace.

CHAPTER 3

How to Build Your Immune System

Seethalakshmi S.

At no point of time in human existence has immunity played such a crucial role as it has in post-COVID times. So, when a team of doctors in Bengaluru began researching on why some succumbed to the deadly virus while lakhs of people across the globe survived it, they found immunity or a stronger thymus gland was one of the primary reasons.

The team found that when there is a loss of thymic function and native T-cells (critical cells to fight foreign invaders), it contributes to weaker immune surveillance. The more these cells regress with ageing, the more susceptible one becomes to the virus attack.

One of the primary reasons young people survived was because of their strong immunity.

So how does one build immunity, that too from a young age? What are the foods to consume? And what kind of lifestyle should one follow to achieve this? As the team of Bengaluru doctors identified the clinical reasons for a strong or weak immune system, a task force constituted by the Union Ayush Ministry (of which Dr Issac Mathai was a part) began parallelly studying why Indians may have a stronger immune system.

In India, our immune system is more resilient, thanks to our good old turmeric, ginger, amla, lemon and honey, which are all antibacterial and which have been a part of our diet from a very young age. And this came into focus once again, during the pandemic. Research all over the world has proved that these foods can fight the viral load in the body and it did for many during COVID. 'These foods that we consciously or unconsciously consume in India in our daily diet are basically antivirus foods,' points out Dr Mathai.

India's Ancient Food

COVID reconfirmed India's ancient food practices, which automatically build the immune system from a young age. The good old concoction of honey, ginger and lime with warm water in the morning as soon as you wake up is what Dr Mathai recommends for building strong immunity. 'It may be difficult for the first few days as some people are used to having coffee as soon as they wake up. But it is only a matter of practice and soon you will get used to it,' says Dr Mathai.

At every step of eating or drinking, Dr Mathai recommends that we always go back to the ancient way of consuming food. For instance, one must not consume the processed juices of various fruits that are sold in the supermarket. Drink homemade juices that contain the pulp, such as orange or pomegranate, which contains three times the amount of antioxidants, and beetroot, carrot and even ginger juices as they contribute to better immunity. Simply consuming healthy foods is not building immunity. 'Everything depends on how it is made. For instance, paneer is good but regularly eating oil-heavy paneer dishes is not,' says Dr Mathai.

The formula to build immunity on a consistent basis is to eat very consciously—to include foods that are rich in antioxidants and vital vitamins. Colourful fruits and vegetables are full of antioxidants. These nutrients guard against free radicals and molecules that can harm your cells. To get a wide range, go for oranges, green peppers, broccoli, kiwi, strawberries, carrots, watermelon, papaya and leafy greens.

In addition to food, there are supplements that boost immunity. Guduchi (Tinospora cordifolia) or Giloy/Amrita is Ayurveda's answer to many infections and fevers. It modulates the immune system by strengthening the body's own defence mechanism in the event of weak immunity due to stress, chronic illness and infections. The anti-inflammatory properties of the herb help counter inflammation, which is often found to weaken the body's defence against invading pathogens such as COVID. It is important that we consciously include this regularly in our food intake so that immunity-building keeps happening. 'And when the virus attacks, it works to protect the body,' says Dr Mathai.

Similarly, Tulasi (Ocimum sanctum) is not only the most revered herb but also has multiple medicinal benefits. Research has proved that Tulasi works against the most common pathogens, namely, bacteria, viruses and fungus, and fights the body's own defences against these infective threats by augmenting immune responses. Besides that, Tulasi can strengthen the immunity of respiratory organs and lower the inflammatory response by modulating pro-inflammatory substances secreted by the cells. Yet another wonder berry is Amla. Rich in vitamin C and other antioxidants, amla can be consumed in various forms, from chyawanprash to chutneys.

Regular inclusion of antioxidants through teas and dietary supplements helps decrease viral replication, reducing rapid viral propagation in the body, especially post COVID. 'The defence mechanism to fight any virus cannot be built in a few days. It's almost a lifetime effort . . . And it must be done consciously so that one is prepared physically when a virus attacks the body,' says Dr Mathai. Ashwagandha, popularly known as Indian ginseng, which regained focus post COVID, has always been held by Ayurvedic texts to nourish tissues that will in turn fight infections. Besides improving nutritional status in the body, ashwagandha also improves haemoglobin levels and muscle strength.

While food is a major component of immunity-building, the body's strength is built slowly and steadily almost every day through good nourishment, adopting a healthy lifestyle, proper sleep and adequate exercise.

With so many pollutants, from our contaminated drinking water to food to air, immune systems tend to get weaker and begin to deteriorate much faster among younger people. A WHO study revealed that a growing number of childhood diseases, including asthma, diabetes and even cancer, have been linked to environmental exposures during prenatal and early postnatal development. And because the immune response plays a critical role in each of these diseases, it is important to consider the effects of toxicants on children's developing immune system (Source: WHO Immune Disease 2011).

Like pollutants, stress can weaken your immune system and therefore the defence system. And that can affect your ability to fight any illness. Building immunity can be done in multiple ways by healing yourself physically and mentally.

Here are some easy steps to build your immunity—The Mathai Formula:

- Unwind every day no matter how much work you have or how busy your day has been.
- Earmark at least one hour for leisure.
- Pets keep you active and are stress-busters.

- Socialize, have good friends and spend time with them regularly so that your life is not just work and work. Research has proved that a good amount of time spent on socializing not only boosts your health but also increases productivity.
- Avoid drinking alcohol as it slowly weakens immunity.
- Kick the cigarette habit. Nicotine kills.
- If you have a social bent of mind, volunteer, teach or pursue your hobby.
- Exercise. Physical activity every single day is the first step to warding away illnesses. Try yoga, aerobics, going to the gym and good old walking or any sport of your choice.
- A good night's sleep is non-negotiable. Lack of sleep can lead to multiple illnesses and destroy immunity.

Feeling good is building immunity. Day by day!

CHAPTER 4

The Perils of Processed Food

Rahul Nandan

We are living in the age of convenience, speed and instant gratification in every possible sense. An easy yet crucial instance is the food we eat. We want our food fresh and tongue-tingling, yet at our convenience and fast. Ready-to-eat products have flooded the markets worldwide. What is important to remember is that convenience always comes at a cost. As highly packaged, calorie-dense processed food continues to become widely available, we keep getting heavier. Almost 40 per cent of the world is overweight or obese, and a staggering number of these are children and adolescents.

Diet-related risk factors such as obesity are among the leading causes of cardiovascular diseases, diabetes and cancer, which together take away forty-one million lives worldwide every year. Are we really aware of the price we pay for the multitude of packaged foodstuffs we pick up every time we visit a supermarket or do we tend to ignore it? We are risking our lives anyway, but let's at least be aware.

Processing food is an ancient technique. Processed food is anything that has been cooked, canned, frozen, packaged, pasteurized, dried or changed in nutritional composition by fortifying, preserving or preparing it in different ways. Any time we cook, bake or prepare food, we are processing food. Processing food isn't something recent to humankind. Our ancestors began to cook food (thermal processing) thousands of years ago. Evidence of grinding grains to make flour, cheesemaking and breadmaking has been found in ancient Israel and Egypt. 'Processing made food easier to digest and chew. Processed foods are convenient and have a longer shelf life. Indeed, they often have many additives that we don't need, but we need not fear all of them,' says Dr Mathai.

The major concern is ultra-processed food

The rising concern is more about the ultra-processed food that we unknowingly consume every day. In the last century, revenue-hungry food companies have driven the trend towards more ultra-processed food—be it flavoured potato chips, sweetened breakfast cereals, sugary carbonated drinks, white bread, fried chicken or artificially flavoured cheese. Ultra-processed foods have ingredients common with industrial food manufacturing, such as hydrogenated oils (trans-fat), high-fructose corn syrup, flavouring agents and emulsifiers. They are cheaper and more convenient but high in calories, salt, sugar and fat. Ultra-processed foods have been known to cause decreased satiety (fullness), increased meal-eating rates (speed), worsening biochemical markers, including inflammation and cholesterol, and more weight gain.

Growing obesity in the world and in India

Rising obesity in the world and related chronic diseases are correlated with a rise in unabated consumption of ultra-processed food. Obesity is among the leading causes of cardiovascular diseases, several kinds of cancer and a majority of type 2 diabetes cases. The worldwide prevalence of obesity has tripled between 1975 and 2016. Around 13 per cent of the world's population was obese in 2016. The growing number of obese children and adolescents in India is a cause for concern. According to a report by the World Obesity Federation, India will have the most number of obese children, twenty-seven million, after China by 2030. The Government of India's Comprehensive National Nutrition Survey that covered 1,12,000 children across thirty states between 2016 and 2018 found that about 5 per cent of children and adolescents between five and nineteen years were overweight. It found the presence of high cholesterol and triglycerides in children and adolescents that increases the risk of heart diseases and other non-communicable diseases, and stressed on the need to aggressively address overweight and obesity. Not long ago, our children mostly ate home-cooked food but junk, packaged food and eating out have now become a way of life. An online survey of over 13,200 kids from 300 schools by the Centre for Science and Environment has revealed the alarming prevalence of packaged, ultra-processed food consumption among urban schoolchildren in India. About 93 per cent of the children eat packaged food, 68 per cent drink sugary beverages more than once a week and 53 per cent consume these products at least once a day. While 56 per cent eat packaged chocolates and ice creams more than twice a week, 53 per cent eat packaged salty food, such as chips and noodles. Almost 27 per cent of schoolchildren eat fast food such as burgers and pizza more than once a week.

Trans-fat and other harmful food trends

In May 2018, WHO called for the global elimination of industrially produced trans-fatty acids (TFA) by 2023 and released an action framework. TFA present in processed food is associated with an increased risk of heart attacks and heart diseases. As of May 2020, best-practice TFA policies—virtually eliminate industrially produced TFA or ban partially hydrogenated oils—are in effect in fourteen countries (8 per cent of the world's population). Canada, the US and, most recently,

Thailand have banned partially hydrogenated oils. Many research reports have warned of the dangers of regularly consuming TFA. Other dangerous food trends include a dramatic increase in food additives such as emulsifiers, gums, flavour enhancers, artificial colours and consistency improvers.

Minimally processed food for good health

A healthy lifestyle and diet are two key factors for a disease-free life. Limiting the intake of processed food that has saturated and trans-fats, sodium and added sugars, and increasing consumption of whole vegetables, legumes, nuts, fruits and water are paramount to tackling obesity and chronic ailments. Trans-fat, salt and sugar are the three biggest enemies of good health. Unsaturated fats (in fish, avocado, nuts, sunflower, soya bean, canola and olive oil) are way healthier than saturated fats (in fatty meat, butter, palm and coconut oil, cream, cheese, ghee and lard) and trans-fats—both industrially produced trans-fats (baked and fried foods, pre-packaged snacks and foods such as frozen pizza, pies, cookies, biscuits, wafers, cooking oils and spreads) and ruminant trans-fats (meat and dairy foods from cows, sheep, goats and camels). Steaming or boiling is preferable to frying when cooking.

To avoid unhealthy weight gain, your intake of saturated fats should be less than 10 per cent and trans-fats less than 1 per cent of your total energy intake. As highly processed foods are becoming widely available and affordable, more people around the world are consuming more salt. High sodium consumption and less potassium intake (less than 3.5 g) causes high BP and increases the risk of heart diseases and strokes. Salt intake can be reduced to less than 5 gm per day by limiting the amount of salt and high-sodium condiments when cooking, limiting the consumption of salty snacks and ultra-processed food and consciously opting for products with lower sodium content. It's not for nothing that sugar is called white poison. Consuming excess sugar increases the risk of tooth decay. 'Calories from foods and drinks high in free sugars lead to unhealthy weight gain and obesity. Free sugars are also known to influence BP and serum lipids, and limiting intake lowers the risk of cardiovascular diseases. Limiting intake of free sugars to less than 10 per cent of total energy intake is part of a healthy diet,' explains Dr Mathai.

Traditional Indian food is holistic and wholesome

The traditional plant-based Indian diet is rich in nutrition and focuses on fresh and whole ingredients. It focuses on a high intake of vegetables, lentils, grains, fruits, dairy and healthy fats and low consumption of meat. A typical Indian meal is mostly balanced with a proper amount of carbs, fats, fibre, proteins and resistant starch. Roots and tubers that are integral to Indian cuisine are rich in whole spices such as turmeric, fenugreek, coriander, ginger, cumin, cardamom, clove, pepper, cinnamon, asafoetida and bay leaves adding rich flavour and powerful nutritional benefits. Using spices to flavour everyday food in India is an ancient practice and promotes good health. Natural sugars such as honey and jaggery are extremely healthy and have been in use for a very long time in Indian kitchens. Traditional natural Indian drinks such as buttermilk, sugarcane juice and coconut water have innumerable health benefits and are safer alternatives to the widely consumed sweetened carbonated beverages. Indigenous tea varieties, including Darjeeling, Assam and Nilgiri teas consumed widely every day, have a host of benefits. Basically, nutritious home-cooked food has been the ingredient of India's healthy diet for ages. Earlier, children mostly ate home-cooked meals and were not exposed to eating out. Obesity, heart ailments, cancer and diabetes were not prevalent in the country's population as they are today. Overindulgence in fried snacks and on-the-shelf processed food in recent times could be the reasons for India's growing prevalence of preventable diseases. Snacks should focus on fresh, whole foods flavoured with herbs and spices. Nuts and seeds, sprouts salad or roasted chickpeas are a few healthy alternatives to fatty fried snacks. So, sticking to traditional Indian home food, including a few food and lifestyle changes in the daily routine coupled with regular exercise could be the key to a healthier and happier life.

The writer is a former senior editor with the *Times of India*.

CHAPTER 5

Time to Go Organic

Be informed, choose the right products.

As more people are becoming conscious about good health, physical exercise and eating the right kind of food have gained prominence in their lives. There is an emerging yet evident shift towards eating healthy and naturally grown food, even if it comes at an extra cost. The organic food industry has witnessed a boom in the past decade with rising consumer awareness and demand, giving birth to innumerable organic food brands and products. And, the COVID-19 pandemic has further pushed the consumer preference in their favour. This shifting preference from comfort food to healthy food has also encouraged more farmers to take to organic ways of farming.

What is organic food?

Food grown without the use of synthetic chemicals such as pesticides and fertilizers and that does not contain genetically modified organisms is 'organic'. To be more precise, it is fresh or processed food that is produced by organic farming methods, which uses fewer or biological pesticides and fertilizers, reduces soil erosion, decreases nitrate leaching into groundwater and surface water, and recycles animal wastes back into the farm. Although organic food products have numerous health and ecological benefits, their yields are low and they cost more. However, the concept of 'organic' is not just limited to 'food without chemicals' but emphasizes the traditional Indian practice of mixed cropping by indigenous farming communities. With large companies entering the organic business for profits, there has been an increasing focus on the monoculture system of agriculture that makes crops vulnerable to pests and compels farmers to grow only a single variety of crop.

Organic food is India's heritage

India has an organic farming legacy spanning thousands of years, and a large part of Indian agricultural produce has been naturally organic for ages. India's traditional agricultural techniques had a deep understanding of nature and always had a collaborative approach between the farmer and the Earth to renew soil vitality in a natural and sustainable manner. Till the Green Revolution in the 1960s, farmers in India largely did not use any pesticides or fertilizers and all produce used to be organic. However, the modern concepts of organic farming were developed in the early 1900s by Sir Albert Howard, F.H. King, Rudolf Steiner and others who believed that the use of animal manures, cover crops, crop rotation and biological pest controls resulted in a better farming system. Having worked in India as an agricultural researcher, Howard gained much inspiration from the traditional and sustainable farming practices and advocated for their adoption in the West. Calls for such environment-friendly and healthy agriculture practices were given by other people in the 1940s and later, such as J.I. Rodale, who was an advocate of sustainable agriculture and organic farming in the US. The organic food demand got a further push in the 1960s but its sales grew steadily from the late twentieth century, which saw enhanced environmental awareness among people, and concerns over the harmful impacts of pesticides and genetically modified crops. India always had a holistic farming system very similar to biodynamic agriculture founded by Rudolf Steiner in 1924, which involved biodynamic production of seeds, preparation of fields and composts, planting and harvesting based on the position of the moon and its relative position within the star signs. There is a need to re-educate farmers in India to return to the old traditional ways of agriculture.

Why is organic food gaining prominence?

A host of factors have led to the growth of the organic food market in recent times. It started with people exploring healthier vegetables and fruits following reports of pesticide residues in them. With more people getting health-conscious and becoming aware of the benefits of organic foods, their popularity has now widened to food grains, pulses, tea, spices and dairy products. As children are more susceptible than adults to diseases caused by pesticide residues in food, parents' preference is gradually shifting to organic products as they feel vegetables, fruits and dairy products produced through conventional farming are no longer safe. There are several worrying reasons for the world's shifting preference for organic foods. These include the widespread use of chemical fertilizers to add nutrients to the soil, sewage sludge being used as fertilizer for vegetables, the alarming presence of chemicals and toxic heavy metals in groundwater and soil, genetic engineering to improve disease or pest resistance or to improve crop yields and feeding antibiotics and growth hormones to livestock. Chemical pesticides and toxic heavy metals are known to cause cancer, developmental delays in infants, reduced sperm quality in men and damage to the liver and kidneys. Antibiotics and growth hormones given to animals directly pass into animal foods such as meat, poultry, fish, eggs and dairy products and from foods to the consumers, leading to the induction of antimicrobial-resistant bacteria in humans. Organically grown food is largely free of all these, is more fresh and nutrient-rich, has higher antioxidants and omega-3 fatty acids and better environmental stability.

The booming organic food industry

The global organic food market grew from $259.06 billion in 2022 to $294.54 billion in 2023 (Organic Food Global Market Report 2023). Retail sales increased in the US from $20.39 billion in 2008 to $47.9 billion in 2019, while sales in Europe reached more than $37 billion (€34.3 billion) in 2017. India's organic food and beverage market has significantly grown in recent years with a prospering middle-class having higher disposable income, rapid urbanization, rising concern for safety and quality of food and a growing section of consumers wanting to embrace a holistic lifestyle. Apart from the country's favourable climatic conditions, the government's policies and schemes supporting organic farming have been pushing growth in this sector like never before. India has the maximum number of organic producers in the world. The country's organic food and beverage retail sales touched $69 million in 2019 and are expected to grow at a rapid pace to reach the $10.75 billion mark by 2025. The country's total area under organic certification is 5.71 million hectares. The increasing land area under certified organic cultivation and production in the coming years is expected to bring down the prices of organic products, making them accessible to a large section of the population. There has been a further surge in the demand for organic food in the wake of the COVID-19 pandemic and the demand for consuming healthy food is here to stay.

What is the right way to buy organic products?

The markets nowadays are flooded with a host of brands claiming to be organic. So, how should a consumer go about buying authentic organic products? Which product is actually organic? How do you identify it? These questions come to the minds of most people who wish to make a switch to healthier, naturally grown food. There are two ways you can procure organic produce: 1) From small-scale farmers who may not be formally certified but who you trust that they grow fresh organic produce, 2) From stores that offer a variety of packed products of certified organic brands. On 1 January 2019, India joined a group of nearly fifty countries that mandates clear and legible consumer-friendly labelling for organic products.

Consumers should make sure that they buy only those products from stores that have the Jaivik Bharat logo and FSSAI (Food Safety and Standard Authority of India) logo license number. In addition, the label may carry the India Organic logo (National Programme for Organic Production certified) or PGS-India Organic logo (PGS-India certified) under whichever system it is certified. The Participatory Guarantee System (PGS) is a locally focused quality assurance system where farmers of neighbouring towns and villages inspect and verify each other's production methods and confirm the adoption of standards. A product may be fake if it claims to be organic but doesn't have the Jaivik Bharat logo. It may have been procured from an unknown farm that neither complies with organic farming practices nor has an FSSAI food licence. So, the next time you go out to buy anything organic, you know what to do. However, it may take consumers some more time to adapt to the current state of the Indian food industry, which is far from perfect, and ensuring high-quality standards will need an extensive testing regime.

CHAPTER 6

Why Gut Health Is Key

How many of us take our gut health seriously? Doctors often do not tell you specifically the details of why gut health (or gut microbiome) is important for your overall health. It helps control digestion and increases your immunity to daily infections too. When there is an imbalance of healthy and unhealthy bacteria in your intestines, you put on weight, have high blood sugar, high cholesterol and a host of other disorders, effectively making you sick. Simply put, your gut balances different bacteria in the body and digests your food. One normally associates bacteria with dirt, isn't it? But did you know that bacteria (the healthy ones) in our body are crucial for our immunity against infections? And that is where our gut or intestinal health matters.

When we speak about the intestines, it is the large intestine that we generally refer to. The large intestine or the colon extends from the ileocecal junction to the anal canal. About 1.5 metres long, it has subdivisions such as the caecum and the appendix, ascending, transverse, descending and sigmoid colon, rectum and the anal canal. Structurally, it is adapted for storage of the faecal matter and for absorption of the fluid and solutes from it. The mucus-secreting cells line it. A major part of the colon presents sacculation. Pouches containing fat also line a major part of the colon.

The intestinal tract is truly teeming with life. Between 100 and 400 different species of microscopic bacteria live in the intestine. With a population of 100 trillion, these bacteria can be 100 times more plentiful than all the other cells of the body combined together. There are both helpful and harmful bacteria in this population. The harmful bacteria try to overpower the helpful and conquer new worlds. The helpful bacteria try to create a balance that is tipped in favour of good health. By creating this balance, they serve as a force in favour of the health of the intestine and thereby the health of the whole body. And that is why maintaining a healthy gut is crucial for wellness.

It is necessary, therefore, for us to strengthen and create a healthy atmosphere for the helpful bacteria. Unfortunately, and more often than not, we seem to be doing the opposite due to our unhealthy eating habits. And this causes serious challenges to our intestinal and overall health. Changing these habits will go a long way in promoting immunity and therefore keeping us healthy.

Effect of antibiotics: One habit that sometimes is lethal to the bacterial world inside us, is the overuse of antibiotics. Often, humans may also consume second-hand antibiotics hidden in meat, poultry and dairy products. The overall effect has been not only the destruction of helpful bacteria but also the introduction of harmful bacteria that are resistant to the antibiotics. And medical science has concluded that when helpful bacteria are destroyed by antibiotics, harmful bacteria may proliferate in the intestines. This creates an imbalance in the bacterial population in our intestines. This imbalance of the bacterial population may then be tipped in favour of thc bad bacteria, resulting in the production of a large variety of virulent infections that may not be contained in the intestine but may infect other areas of the body.

Damage to the intestinal wall: In addition to preserving and promoting a healthy bacterial population in the intestine, it is important to maintain the health of the structure where the bacteria live, which is the intestinal lining itself.

So how do we harm the intestinal wall? By excess consumption of alcohol (or alcohol abuse), consumption of raw eggs, raw oysters and other foods (that may produce bacterial infections in the intestines), consumption of aspirin and other painkillers that damage the intestinal lining, use of broad-spectrum antibiotics leading to diarrhoea and yeast infections.

Diet and intestinal health: Today, the average diet of an individual consists of highly refined and processed food, which is harmful to intestinal health. Processed and refined food contains excess sugars and fats and is deficient in nutrition compared to wholefoods, unprocessed foods and fibre. So, when processed food/diet is consumed, it leads to irregular bowel movements indicating intestinal ill-health. This food/diet works to bring in an imbalance in the bacterial population in the intestine by supporting the overgrowth of unhealthy bacteria and the proliferation of yeast or fungal organisms. Eventually, this leads to the deterioration of the intestinal wall.

How to have a good gut or intestine

For long, people have supported intestinal health by consuming natural probiotics in the form of cultured dairy products such as yogurt, kefir and fermented milk.

Probiotics: The term 'probiotics' refers to organisms and or supportive substances that beneficially affect the balance of the intestinal bacteria. The most important among these is the Lactobacillus acidophilus and Bifidobacterium infantis. Their supportive properties include the production of organic acids that inhibit the growth of certain undesirable bacteria and the promotion of a healthy intestinal wall, to mention a few.

Prebiotics

Prebiotics are specialized plant fibres. They act like fertilizers that stimulate the growth of healthy bacteria in the gut. They include whole grains, bananas, soya bean, onions and garlic. Prebiotics are found in many fruits and vegetables, especially those that contain complex carbohydrates, such as fibre and resistant starch. These carbs are not digestible by your body, so they pass through the digestive system to become food for bacteria and other microbes.

- Miso soup
- Sauerkraut
- Kimchi
- Kombucha
- Kefir (dairy and non-dairy)
- Pickled vegetables

Probiotics

Probiotics are different in that they contain live organisms, usually specific strains of bacteria that directly add to the population of healthy microbes in your gut. Like prebiotics, you can take probiotics through both food and supplements. Probably the most common probiotic food is yogurt. Others include:

- Bananas
- Onions
- Garlic
- Berries
- Legumes
- Beans
- Peas

- Oats
- Asparagus
- Dandelion greens
- Leeks
- Apple skin

Dietary fibre is also important. Independent studies at Soukya showed that adding fibre to the liquid diet reduced the number of bacteria crossing the intestinal wall and getting into the circulation by 90 per cent. Complex carbohydrates, known as fructooligosaccharides, are fibre, as in that humans do not digest it, but it serves as food for the healthy bacteria.

Certain bioactive proteins are another class of supportive substances that qualify as probiotics. They are produced in the body naturally or can be obtained from various foods. They help maintain the balance of healthy intestinal bacteria by inhibiting those that are unhealthy. Lactoferrin is an iron-binding protein. It prevents bad bacteria from getting the iron it needs to live. Lactoperoxidase is a protein enzyme that, in various ways, damages the unhealthy bacteria. Certain globulin protein is derived from dairy as they prevent unhealthy bacteria from attaching to the intestinal wall, making them easy to eliminate.

Additionally, it is important to make sure that a good diet includes pure water. The use of tap water from a municipal source contains chlorine, which may destroy the healthy bacteria in the intestine.

Dr Mathai's recommendations for optimal intestinal health

- ❖ Avoid the use of broad-spectrum antibiotics and NSAIDs as much as possible.
- ❖ Avoid a refined, sugar- and fat-rich, fibre-poor diet, and the overconsumption of alcohol and chlorinated water.
- ❖ Eat a diet rich in whole, unprocessed, nutritionally adequate foods and fibre. Also consider adding fibre like fructooligosaccharides to your diet, such as onion, garlic, asparagus, banana, wheat, tomatoes, artichokes and many others.
- ❖ Supplement the diet with scientifically proven, high-quality, healthful bacterial products, such as Bifidobacterium infantis and the Lactobacillus acidophilus NCFM, which is a probiotic strain available in conventional foods (milk, yogurt, and toddler formula).
- ❖ Consume a diet rich in, or supplement the diet with, probiotic proteins such as lactoperoxidase, lactoferrin and globulin proteins.
- ❖ Consume vegetarian sources of fibre, such as green leafy vegetables, raw salads and fruits.
- ❖ Consume protein-rich foods, such as green gram, chickpea and soya.

Colonic irrigation

This is a natural hydrotherapeutic technique where 45–50 litres of water are passed through the colon over a period of thirty to forty-five minutes, which enables the accumulated matter in the colon to get out of the body, thereby improving intestinal hygiene. Most of the unhealthy bacteria could also be eliminated through this technique. This is a very safe technique, which could be planned according to the individual's needs.

Curd

The ubiquitous dahi or curd is indeed a superfood. And its popularity is not only due to various health claims and therapeutic effects but also to its sensory properties. The primary sensory attributes of yogurt include texture, colour and flavour. Lactic acid growth depends on location, weather and main flavour component, which is made by starter bacteria during curd production and storage. This compound is responsible for the specific acidity of fermented milk. The flavour components of yogurt are affected because of these modifications, which is considered the safest, healthiest and natural form one can consume on a daily basis.

Curd (Dahi) and Yogurt: What's the difference?

Dahi, or curd, is made with lactobacillus. Although the same process of fermentation is followed for yogurt, another bacteria is added in it called streptococcus thermophilus, apart from lactobacillus.

More or less, both of them do the same thing since both are rich in probiotics. Yogurt is a dairy product that is created by the bacterial fermentation of milk. Curd is a dairy product that is manufactured by curdling milk with certain edible acidic substances. The fermentation of milk in yogurt is caused by using bacteria known as 'yogurt cultures' that consists of Lactobacillus bulgaricus and Streptococcus thermophilus.

Benefits of having curd:

Curd is good for the immune system

There are various kinds of components that benefit the body. Curd is one of the best probiotic foods, which has live microorganisms present in it that are needed by the human body. The power and strength provided by curd to the metabolism results in enhanced immunity. This immunity allows the body to fight various microorganisms and stay healthy.

Curd is good for weight loss

People trying to reduce weight should include curd in their diet plan. With the immense amount of calcium availability, curd helps to fight obesity. Calcium restricts the creation of cortisol, which leads the body away from weight increase. So, to fight cortisol, a person should regularly have a certain amount of curd. About 18 ounces (510 grams) is enough to provide the necessary amount of calcium in the body. There is some evidence that yogurt with active cultures helps certain gastrointestinal conditions, including lactose intolerance, constipation, diarrhoea, colon cancer, inflammatory bowel disease and H. pylori infection.

So go for the curd!

CHAPTER 7

Sleep and Why It's Important

What has sleep got to do with COVID? And how does sleep build your immunity against a viral attack? When doctors all over the world began to ponder why certain patients recovered from the deadly coronavirus while some succumbed, they found that the latter had inadequate cytokines (a powerful immune protein in our body). Simply put, when there is a viral attack on our bodies, these proteins are released by our immune system to fight the virus. And the lack of these proteins will make us weak before the virus.

Research has proved that during sleep, your immune system releases proteins called cytokines, some of which help promote sleep. Now, sleep deprivation may decrease the production of these protective cytokines and reduce our ability to fight back the virus when it attacks. 'The infection-fighting antibodies and cells are reduced during periods when you don't get enough sleep. And consistent lack of sleep weakens the immune system,' says Dr Mathai, adding, 'It's fine to miss sleep once in a while, maybe during examinations or to complete a project. But consistently disturbing sleep hours is dangerous and increases the risk of obesity, diabetes, cardiovascular diseases and now COVID.

As researchers continue to fill in the gaps about what exactly is going on biologically while we sleep, we also need to regain the deeper connection with ourselves that sleep can bring us every night. For example, if you need to be up by 6 a.m., you should consider winding down before 11 p.m. The amount of sleep you need each day will change over the course of your life.

Although sleep needs vary from person to person and from age group to age group, there is no conclusive study on the debate that some people need less sleep compared to others. The recent American Academy of Sleep Medicine (AASM) study revealed that infants (4–12 months) need 12–16 hours of sleep, children in the age group 1–2 years need 11–14 hours, children in the age group of 3–5 years need 10–13 hours (which includes short naps), children in the age group 6–12 years need 9–12 hours. And as they grow up, their sleep requirement decreases. Teens (13–18 years) require 8–10 hours while adults (18 years upwards) need 7–8 hours. So any continuous reduction in the number of hours in each of these age groups adds up to sleep deficiency and therefore, illness and low immunity to fight disease. 'The body gets weaker and weaker. Though you may not collapse initially due to lack of sleep, eventually it will catch up and one day the tired body gives up,' says Dr Mathai.

It is crucial not to build sleep debt. For example, if you lose two to three hours of sleep each night, you'll have a sleep debt of 14–21 hours after a week. And if this sleep debt becomes a routine, the body starts showing signs of deprivation. And this can range from day-long fatigue, lack of attention, losing temper easily, loss of appetite, etc. Doctors say these are all signals the body is giving out to say, rectify the inadequate sleep and just rest. Ignoring the signals can lead to serious illness.

So, do short naps during the day help? Yes, they do. They relieve body fatigue and get you back on your feet immediately. But napping does not put the body on a complete rest or repair mode simply because it is short (fifteen to thirty minutes). Nothing substitutes a good seven to eight-hour complete rest to the body during the night-time.

A techie working for an MNC asked Dr Mathai if he could skip sleep during the week and make up for it during the weekends when he was not working. The answer was NO. While it is okay to rest more during the weekends, it is not good to sleep for three or four hours during the weekdays and sleep for twenty hours during the weekends. That will disturb the sleep–wake rhythms that will eventually affect your immunity. If you are a shift worker or doctor on call or nurse, then you need to work around your wake hours and stay in sync with your sleep needs. At no cost should people in these professions lack adequate sleep.

Sleep deficiency and disorders can be costly. Untreated sleep disorders are associated with a growing number of health problems ranging from heart disease, high BP, stroke, diabetes, obesity and even certain cancers. On the other hand, if you are feeling ill or fatigued even after getting the adequate hours of sleep, then you must consult your doctor for any other hidden ailment.

What can you do?

- Maintain a sleep diary for a couple of weeks that will tell you if you are sleeping enough.
- Note down the time you hit the bed and when you wake up. Keep it uniform. Say if you sleep at 10 p.m. and wake up at 6 a.m., stick to this at least during the observation period. This will help identify the real problem, if any.
- Note down how you feel after waking up. Feeling good and rested?
- Also note down if you are feeling fatigued or sleepy during the day.
- Go to bed and wake up at the same time every day. Try to keep the same sleep schedule on weeknights and weekends as far as possible.
- Avoid watching TV or the computer screen at least an hour before your bedtime. This will help the body relax and sleep easily.
- Stick to a light meal for dinner. Eating too much can lead to difficulty in sleeping especially at night-time.
- Caffeine and nicotine have a huge impact on sleep habits. Avoid nicotine (cigarettes) and caffeine (soda, coffee, tea and chocolate) to ensure uninterrupted sleep.
- Sleep often is the first thing that busy people squeeze out of their schedules. Stop that now and respect your body's plea to rest.

CHAPTER 8

Lifestyle Modification for Daily Wellness

What are lifestyle changes?

Lifestyle changes are behaviour modifications or habit changes that encourage positive changes in your life. These are a fundamental component to any wellness programme.

Examples of lifestyle habits include:

- Sleep: The average adult should try to sleep seven to nine hours each night. During restful sleep, your body has time to regenerate and recharge. This time is integral to the success of making a lifestyle change. Lack of sleep can result in irritability, cravings and fatigue, all of which can derail a successful lifestyle change.

- **Water:** Hydration is the key to most of your bodily functions. Without staying hydrated, neither your body nor your mind will be working with the lifestyle change process. So, drink sufficient water regularly.
- **Stress:** By taking care of your body, you are naturally signalling to your brain that your overall stress levels can decrease. A new habit can reinforce your stress management system and will ultimately lead to overall stress management success. Focus on finding manageable habits you can integrate into your daily routine. You can build on those strong core routines as you continue to reach for your long-term goals.
- **Consumption:** Nutrition is an important element of the puzzle. When we charge our body with healthy ingredients, we can focus on building and maintaining healthy habits. When we fuel up with junk food, we will inevitably crash and fall off the lifestyle change wagon. Focus on finding healthy replacements for junk food that you can actually sustain.
- **Exercise:** Staying active affects your physical and mental health. By finding fun ways to stay active, you provide additional endorphins that help your brain and body function at peak performance.
- **Sun bath:** As the name suggests, sunbathing simply refers to sitting or lying in the sun. As you might already know, sunlight is the primary source of vitamin D, a vital nutrient, which your

body produces when exposed to sunrays. This particular nutrient is great for bones, muscles and the immune system. The benefits of sunbathing are generally linked to vitamin D. Only fifteen minutes of exposure early in the morning is sufficient. You must know that sunbathing is considered a part of yoga (Surya Namaskar) because of its healing properties. Sunbathing builds stronger bones, helps with depression, helps you relax, boosts immunity, gives you better sleep and is good for Alzheimer's patients.

Making changes to these habits can create long-lasting effects on your personal well-being.

How to make healthy lifestyle changes

Healthy habit formation requires practice and routine. After approximately twenty-one days, engaging in a new behaviour begins to feel natural. This means you could form a healthy habit in just three weeks.

Habit replacement is the most effective method for making lifestyle changes.

There are three primary categories of lifestyle changes. They are:

- **Psychological changes:** This includes changes to your attitude, your mood and the way you manage stress. To make healthy psychological changes, you may find it useful to join a support group or keep a journal.

- **Behavioural changes:** While all lifestyle changes are technically behavioural, this category refers to things like your sleeping habits, activity level and planning efforts.
- **Dietary changes:** Making healthy changes to your diet can help you lose weight, balance hormone levels and manage pain. These changes will include controlling portion sizes, drinking more water and following a nutritious diet.

Changing just one behaviour at a time can lead to lasting changes in your life and is much less intimidating than attempting to completely overhaul your current lifestyle.

Find your why

Finding your why is the single greatest thing you can do if you want to make your lifestyle change easy. By discovering what your deepest goal is, you can stay motivated and positive during the process. When setting goals, it is helpful to focus on overall health and lifestyle.

Notes

Foreword

1 Marcin Barański et al., 'Higher Antioxidant and Lower Cadmium Concentrations and Lower Incidence of Pesticide Residues in Organically Grown Crops: A Systematic Literature Review and Meta-Analyses,' Cambridge University Press, https://www.cambridge.org/core/journals/british-journal-of-nutrition/article/div-classtitlehigher-antioxidant-and-lower-cadmium-concentrations-and-lower-incidence-of-pesticide-residues-in-organically-grown-crops-a-system-atic-literature-review-and-meta-analysesdiv/33F09637EAE6C4ED119E0C4BFFE2D5B1.

2 Indira Rathore, Vandana Shiva, Esther Thomas and J.C. Tarafdar, 'A Comparison on Soil Biological Health on Continuous Organic and Inorganic Farming,' MedCrave, https://medcraveonline.com/HIJ/a-comparison-on-soil-biological-health-on-continuous-organic-and-inorganic-farming.html.

Chapter 1: The A–Z of Common Ailments

1 Stephen Hochschuler, 'What You Need to Know About Sciatica', 5 June 2019, https://www.spine-health.com/conditions/sciatica/what-you-need-know-about-sciatica#vh_footnotes

Chapter 4: The Perils of Processed Food

1 'Obesity and Overweight', 9 June 2021, World Health Organization. https://www.who.int/news-room/fact-sheets/detail/obesity-and-overweight#:~:text=In%20 2016%2C%2039%25%20of%20adults,tripled%20 between%201975%20and%202016
2 'Countdown to 2023', WHO report on global trans fat elimination 2020, https://apps.who.int/iris/bitstream/handle/10665/334170/9789240010178-eng.pdf
3 Nicola Temple, '5 things you probably didn't know about processed food', *Science Focus*, 29 November 2019.
4 'Obesity and Overweight', World Health Organization.
5 Sonam Taneja, Amit Khurana, 'Availability of Junk Food Is Changing Children's Diet in India', DownToEarth, 15 August 2017, https://www.downtoearth.org.in/news/health/spoilt-for-choice-58417
6 'Healthy Diet', World Health Organization, 29 April 2020, https://www.who.int/news-room/fact-sheets/detail/healthy-diet
7 Ibid.
8 Ibid.

Chapter 5: Time to Go Organic

1 Leslie A. Duram, 'Organic Food', Britannica, https://www.britannica.com/topic/organic-food#ref1261800

2 Raoul Adamchak, 'Organic Farming', Britannica, https://www.britannica.com/topic/organic-farming

3 Parul Abrol, 'The Organic Food Revolution: A Nightmare for India?', *The Diplomat*, 21 September 2018.

4 Raoul Adamchak, 'Organic Farming', Britannica.

5 Amanda Macmillan and Julia Naftulin, '4 Science-Backed Health Benefits of Eating Organic', *Time*, 27 July 2017, https://time.com/4871915/health-benefits-organic-food/

6 Raoul Adamchak, 'Organic Farming', Britannica.

7 Ankit Chandra and Mark Rosmann, 'Indian Organic Foods Market Report', USDA Foreign Agricultural Service, GAIN, 15 June 2020, https://apps.fas.usda.gov/newgainapi/api/Report/DownloadReportByFileName?fileName=Indian%20Organic%20Foods%20Market%20Report_New%20Delhi_India_06-08-2020

8 'A Glance at Some Interesting Facts', Jaivik Bharat, https://jaivikbharat.fssai.gov.in/

